FIFTY STATES

MINN.

WIS.

MICH.

ME.

N.Y. VT.

N.H.

MASS.

CONN. R.I.

PA.

N.J.

IA.

ILL.

IND.

OHIO

Appalachian Mountains

W. VA. VA.

MD.

DEL.

NEB.

MO.

KY.

N.C.

KAN.

TENN.

OKLA.

ARK.

S.C.

MISS.

ALA. GA.

LA.

FLA.

HAWAII

0   100

★ DISTRICT OF COLUMBIA

0   500

ALL ABOUT OUR 50 STATES

Here are good reading, intriguing facts, and useful information about each state of the Union. Special sections give fuller coverage to our two newest states, Alaska and Hawaii.

In this book, you can find the capital of every state, its area and population, its rank compared with other states, the year of its admission to the Union, time zones across the nation, the growth of the United States shown in maps—all this and much, much more.

All About Our 50 States is generously illustrated with 65 maps, 47 photographs, and 51 drawings.

ALL ABOUT
OUR
50 STATES

★ ★

BY MARGARET RONAN

DRAWINGS BY
WILLIAM MEYERRIECKS

MAPS BY
FRANK RONAN

REVISED EDITION

RANDOM HOUSE, NEW YORK

Copyright © 1962, 1978 by Random House, Inc., Copyright © 1961 by Scholastic Magazines, Inc. All rights reserved under International and Pan-American Copyright Conventions. Published in the United States by Random House, Inc., New York, and simultaneously in Canada by Random House of Canada Limited, Toronto.

Library of Congress Cataloging in Publication Data
Ronan, Margaret. All about our 50 States. Includes index. SUMMARY: Presents a compendium of facts, figures, and information concerning each state in the Union. 1. United States—Description and travel—1960– Juvenile literature. [1. United States—Description and travel] I. Meyerriecks, William. II. Ronan, Frank. III Title. E169.02.R63 1978 973 78–16658 ISBN 0–394–80244–6 ISBN 0–394–90244–0 lib. bdg. Manufactured in the United States of America 1 2 3 4 5 6 7 8 9 10

All About Our 50 States is an expanded edition of an Arrow Book Club selection published by Scholastic Book Services under a different title. This book contains approximately 2,300 words and 15 photographs not included in Scholastic's Arrow Book Club edition. This edition is published by arrangement with Scholastic Book Services, a division of Scholastic Magazines, Inc.

Every effort has been made to have the text of this book checked by the appropriate authorities in each state. The editors wish to express their appreciation for the many helpful suggestions that they have received from coast to coast.

Photograph credits (left to right, top to bottom): page 105, U.S. Forest Service, Fred Machetanz; 107, U.S. Fish and Wildlife Service; 108, 109, Western Electric; 110, United Air Lines; 112, Bernice P. Bishop Museum; 113, Dole Corporation; 114, Hawaii Visitors Bureau; 115, U.S. Geological Survey; 116, United Press International, Office of War Information Photo by Palmer, Maine Highway Commission; 117, Log Cabin Syrup, General Dynamics; 118, Photography for Industry, Wheaton (from Monkmeyer), photo from *U.S. News and World Report;* 119, U.S. Steel, Monkmeyer Press Photo Service; 120, Liama Druskis from Editorial Photocolor Archives, Live Stock Photo Company, Allis-Chalmers International; 121, Pace (from Monkmeyer), General Motors; 122, Greene Line Steamers, Inc., International Harvester Company, Kentucky Chamber of Commerce, Standard Oil of New Jersey; 123, Twentieth Century Fund, Philip Gendreau; 124, U.S. Bureau of Reclamation, U.S. Air Force, Landwehr (from Monkmeyer); 125, U.S. Geological Survey and the Atomic Energy Commission, U.S. Department of Interior; 126, National Film Board of Canada (from the Canadian Consulate), Editorial Photocolor Archives, Hawaiian Pineapple Company, U.S. Fish and Wildlife Service; 127, Black Star (left bottom).

CONTENTS

MEET YOUR STATES

Alabama to Florida   2
Georgia to Maine   22
Maryland to New Hampshire   42
New Jersey to Rhode Island   62
South Carolina to Wyoming   82

OUR TWO NEWEST STATES

Alaska   104
Hawaii   110

ACROSS THE UNITED STATES IN PHOTOGRAPHS

New England   116
Middle Atlantic States   118
Middle West   120
Southern States   122
Mountain States   124
Pacific Coast   126

Fifty States Under One Flag   128
How America Grew: A Map Story   129
Set Your Clock: Time Zones of the U.S.   132
State Birds and Flowers   133
State Areas and Populations   134
Did You Know?   136
Index   138

STATES AND THEIR ABBREVIATIONS

	Old	New*		Old	New*
Alabama	Ala.	AL	Montana	Mont.	MT
Alaska	None	AK	Nebraska	Nebr.	NE
Arizona	Ariz.	AZ	Nevada	Nev.	NV
Arkansas	Ark.	AR	New Hampshire	N.H.	NH
California	Calif.	CA	New Jersey	N.J.	NJ
Colorado	Colo.	CO	New Mexico	N. Mex.	NM
Connecticut	Conn.	CT	New York	N.Y.	NY
Delaware	Del.	DE	North Carolina	N.C.	NC
Florida	Fla.	FL	North Dakota	N. Dak.	ND
Georgia	Ga.	GA	Ohio	None	OH
Hawaii	None	HI	Oklahoma	Okla.	OK
Idaho	None	ID	Oregon	Oreg.	OR
Illinois	Ill.	IL	Pennsylvania	Pa.	PA
Indiana	Ind.	IN	Rhode Island	R.I.	RI
Iowa	None	IA	South Carolina	S.C.	SC
Kansas	Kans.	KS	South Dakota	S. Dak.	SD
Kentucky	Ky.	KY	Tennessee	Tenn.	TN
Louisiana	La.	LA	Texas	Tex.	TX
Maine	Me.	ME	Utah	None	UT
Maryland	Md.	MD	Vermont	Vt.	VT
Massachusetts	Mass.	MA	Virginia	Va.	VA
Michigan	Mich.	MI	Washington	Wash.	WA
Minnesota	Minn.	MN	West Virginia	W. Va.	WV
Mississippi	Miss.	MS	Wisconsin	Wis.	WI
Missouri	Mo.	MO	Wyoming	Wyo.	WY

* These new abbreviations were approved in 1963 by the Post Office Department. They will gradually replace the old abbreviations.

ALL ABOUT OUR 50 STATES

TENNESSEE

Muscle Shoals

TENNESSEE

RIVER

Birmingham

ALABAMA

MISSISSIPPI

GEORGIA

★ Montgomery

N

Mobile

FLORIDA

GULF OF MEXICO

0   100

• This monument to the boll weevil stands in the town of Enterprise. It was placed in the public square by Alabama farmers. The inscription reads: "In profound appreciation of the boll weevil and what it has done to herald prosperity."

ALABAMA

"The Heart of Dixie" became the 22nd State, 1819

IT is 1910 in Alabama. The fields are planted with cotton—nothing but cotton. Then one day the boll weevils swarm in. When they are gone there is no cotton left. There are no crops to sell. What were Alabama's farmers to do? How could they make a living? They solved the problem by planting a variety of crops— corn and hay, tobacco and peanuts, sugar cane and fruit.

Alabama still grows more cotton than any other crop, but the boll weevil taught the farmers a valuable lesson—not to depend on a single crop. The farmers were so grateful they built a monument to the cotton-eating bug.

In northern Alabama, factories turn Alabama cotton into cloth and cottonseed oil. Where does the power come from that turns the machines? From the mighty Tennessee River! Once the surging waters of the Tennessee used to flood homes and farms. Today a series of dams prevents flooding by storing the extra water.

The furnaces of Birmingham blast night and day, making steel from iron ore and limestone. Birmingham produces so much steel it is called the "Pittsburgh of the South."

Pine forests that cover half the state echo to the shouts of loggers and crashing trees. The trees that are cut down are shipped to mills to be made into furniture, pulp and paper.

The people of Alabama can't use all the goods they themselves produce. Surplus goods are sent to Mobile, Alabama's port on the Gulf of Mexico. There the goods are shipped to faraway places all over the world.

ALASKA

"The Last Frontier" became the 49th State, 1959

OUR 49th state is a place of contrasts. Most of Alaska is still a wild frontier, yet you can also find skyscraper apartment houses. An Eskimo puts out to sea in a whaleskin boat, but the boat may be powered by an outboard motor. And a dog team pulls a sled over snow and ice—hurrying to a modern airport.

Alaska is not all snow and ice, however, even in winter. And in summer, the temperature in Fairbanks sometimes soars to 100 degrees. Here truck gardens grow strawberries as big as plums, and the sun—shining until late evening—can give you a sunburn. The most northerly point in the U.S. is Point Barrow. Here, from May through July, you can fish all night by the light of the midnight sun.

Alaska is BIG—twice as big as Texas. North America's highest mountain is in Alaska—Mt. McKinley, 20,320 feet tall. Malaspina Glacier is as big as Rhode Island! And there is a volcano with a crater six miles across. This volcano Aniakchak, is near the Valley of Ten Thousand Smokes. Steam and smoke puffing from craters all over this strange valley make it look like some giant's kitchen.

Salmon fishing is the most important industry, but gold is what comes to mind when most people think of Alaska. With the discovery of gold in the late 1800's prospectors poured into Alaska's wilderness. Many of them settled there.

Today Alaska produces more platinum than any other state. Alaskans cut timber for their pulp mills, pump oil from under the sea, and produce many beautiful furs.

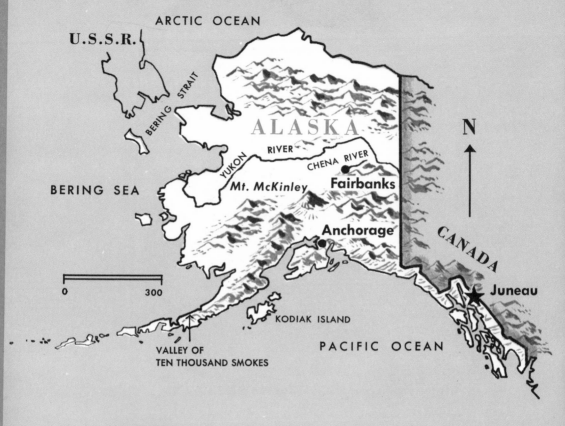

ARCTIC OCEAN

U.S.S.R.

BERING SEA

ALASKA

YUKON RIVER

CHENA RIVER

Mt. McKinley

Fairbanks

Anchorage

N

CANADA

Juneau

0   300

KODIAK ISLAND

VALLEY OF
TEN THOUSAND SMOKES

PACIFIC OCEAN

• Huge brown Kodiak bears live on Kodiak Island, south of the Alaska mainland. These bears are the world's largest meat-eating land animals. They may stand ten feet tall and weigh as much as a ton and a half. They enjoy eating salmon and get their dinner by sweeping the fish out of the streams with their paws.

UTAH

NEVADA

NEW MEXICO

Grand Canyon

PAINTED DESERT

COLORADO RIVER

CALIFORNIA

ARIZONA

Phoenix ★

Tucson ●

N

0   100

MEXICO

• These Hopi Indians perform the ancient tribal Feather Dance. Hopi Indians still live in the little villages called *pueblos* that their ancestors occupied for hundreds of years.

ARIZONA

"Grand Canyon State" became the 48th State, 1912

CACTUS, cowboys and Indians. Arizona has them in abundance. A whole *forest* of cactus trees grows near Phoenix. Cowboys? Thousands of them work on ranches. Indians? More Indians live in Arizona than in any other state.

But if some parts of Arizona remind you of a TV western, others take you right into the Atomic Age. Uranium is mined in the hillsides. And in the desert, factories make parts for jets.

Arizona is a land of natural wonders. Its forests and canyons tell exciting stories of the early days of the world. The Grand Canyon is one of the most awesome spectacles on earth. For centuries the Colorado River cut its way through layers of rock. As the river sank, it left red and yellow rock walls *a mile high* on either side. The Grand Canyon is so deep it has different climates at different levels.

The Painted Desert has rainbow-colored sands. And Meteor Crater is a gigantic hole, 600 feet deep and a mile wide—made by a huge meteor that crashed millions of years ago. There's a spooky forest in Arizona, too, that was alive centuries ago. Today it is the Petrified Forest, its fallen logs and stunted trees all solid stone.

Arizona is rich in natural resources as well as in natural wonders. About half our nation's copper comes from Arizona's mines. Gold is mined here, too, as well as lead and silver.

Arizona is rich in perfect weather, too. The dry and sunny climate is one reason why the population has tripled since the end of World War II.

ARKANSAS

"Land of Opportunity" became the 25th State, 1836

IT was not gold that the Spanish explorer de Soto found in Arkansas, but "magic water." For there are more health-giving mineral springs in Arkansas than anywhere else in the U.S. The Lewis and Clark Expedition noted these springs in 1804. And no matter how fiercely the Indians fought one another, they kept Hot Springs as neutral territory which all tribes could use.

Mammoth Spring is one of the largest springs in the world. The two hundred million gallons of water that gush forth from Mammoth each day are stored in two dams and used to create electric power.

The earth of Arkansas yields more than "magic water." It is rich, too, in minerals, such as bauxite. Nearly all the U.S. output of this important aluminum ore is mined in Arkansas. Along the Arkansas River are vast coal fields. And the only diamond mine in North America is near Murfreesboro.

Though much of the state is forest land, and lumbering is the most important industry, Arkansas is mainly a farming state.

Arkansas has a varied landscape. To the east are cotton plantations, like those in Alabama or Mississippi. To the southwest, cattle ranches and grazing range look like land in Texas. And the bayous, swamps and moss-hung oaks in the southeast are much like those in Louisiana.

The next time you write on the blackboard, think of Chalk Bluff, Arkansas. This hill contains enough chalk to keep your class supplied for hundreds of years.

MISSOURI

Ozark Mountains

↑
MAMMOTH SPRING

Fort
Smith

OKLAHOMA

Hot Springs ● ● Little
Rock

ARKANSAS RIVER

● Murfreesboro

ARKANSAS

TEXAS

LOUISIANA

MISSISSIPPI

TENNESSEE

N
↑

0   100

• Spanish explorer Hernando de Soto, seeking gold, was the first white man to explore Arkansas. After sighting the Mississippi River, in 1541, his expedition crossed into Arkansas and explored the Ozark Mountains.

OREGON

NEVADA

SACRAMENTO RIVER

★ Sacramento
San
Francisco ● Oakland

SAN JOAQUIN RIVER

DEATH
VALLEY
DESERT

CALIFORNIA

PACIFIC OCEAN

MOJAVE
DESERT

N

Los Angeles

ARIZONA

0   100

MEXICO

• Californians can boast of
having more people than any
other state. They used to boast
that Golden Gate Bridge in San Francisco had the
world's longest single bridge span. That was true
until the Verrazano-Narrows Bridge was built in
New York.

CALIFORNIA

"The Golden State" became the 31st State, 1850

"EL DORADO" ("The Golden Place"), cried the Spanish explorers in 1535.

"*Kun Shan*" ("The Golden Hills"), murmured Chinese workers, gazing at the hills of San Francisco more than three hundred years later.

"GOLD!" shouted prospectors in 1848, and the famous California gold rush began.

There's another kind of gold in California—golden sunshine that helps to grow the greatest fruit and vegetable crops in the U.S. There's "black gold" too—crude oil bubbling out of the ground from hundreds of oil fields.

California is, after New York, the leading producer of manufactured goods. Automobile and aircraft production are the state's leading industries.

California is full of natural wonders. Death Valley, 282 feet below sea level—is the lowest land in the country. "General Sherman" can be found in Sequoia National Park. The General is not a soldier, but the world's oldest and biggest tree.

There's a special kind of stargazing you can do in Los Angeles—watching Hollywood movie stars at work. In Los Angeles, too, are California's first "citizens"—fossils of the Ice Age. They were discovered in the tar pits of La Brea—one of the richest finds of prehistoric fossils ever unearthed.

Farther north, on the seacoast, is the Vandenburg Air Base, where guided missiles and satellites blast off. You travel quickly in California—from the Ice Age to the Space Age.

COLORADO

"The Centennial State" became the 38th State, 1876

IN 1820, Major Stephen Long, exploring Colorado, called its vast plains the "Great American Desert." He could not know that someday Colorado farms would yield rich crops of wheat, corn and sugar beets. For today the waters of the Platte and Arkansas rivers irrigate this desert. And water even flows to the land through tunnels in the mountain wall of the Continental Divide.

From a plane, the Continental Divide looks like a giant's backbone. The Divide zigzags north to south through the entire Rocky Mountain Range. Rain falling on the western slope of the Divide flows to the Pacific. Rain falling on the eastern slope ends in the Atlantic Ocean.

This state has half of the highest mountains in the U.S., and once the Colorado Rockies seemed impossible to cross. Today roads wind around the peaks, bridges cross the gorges, trains rush through tunnels blasted into the rock.

On the edge of the mountains at mile-high Denver, gold was discovered in 1858. The next year prospectors thronged to Colorado. This gold rush changed the history of Colorado and made it a state—for towns sprang up and railroads were built. Settlers found not only gold, but other minerals—silver, copper, coal, and oil. Some gave up treasure-hunting and started farms and cattle ranches instead.

Colorado is still a great mining state, and now its hills yield a new kind of treasure—uranium, raw material for atomic energy.

12

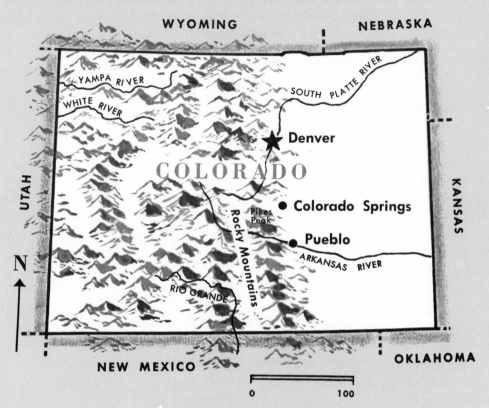

WYOMING   NEBRASKA

YAMPA RIVER

WHITE RIVER

SOUTH PLATTE RIVER

★ Denver

UTAH

COLORADO

● Colorado Springs

Pikes Peak

● Pueblo

KANSAS

Rocky Mountains

ARKANSAS RIVER

N

RIO GRANDE

NEW MEXICO   OKLAHOMA

0   100

• Pikes Peak is Colorado's most famous mountain. It was named for Zebulon Pike, who tried to climb it in 1806. "Pikes Peak or Bust" became the slogan of gold seekers off to join the Colorado gold rush, which reached its height by the end of 1859. The mountain is part of the Colorado Rockies and towers 14,110 feet above sea level.

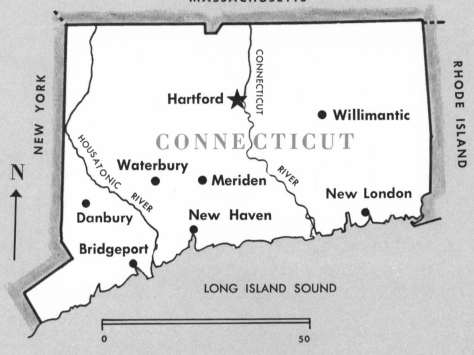

MASSACHUSETTS

NEW YORK

RHODE ISLAND

N

Hartford ★

Willimantic

CONNECTICUT RIVER

HOUSATONIC RIVER

CONNECTICUT

Waterbury

Meriden

New London

Danbury

New Haven

Bridgeport

LONG ISLAND SOUND

0   50

• Charter Oak was a large tree which once stood in Hartford. It was used as a hiding place in 1687 for Connecticut's own charter for self-government. Joseph Wadsworth hid the valuable charter in the tree to keep it from being seized by the British governor. Charter Oak blew down in a storm in 1856, but a monument marks the spot where it once stood.

CONNECTICUT

"The Nutmeg State" became the 5th State, 1788

AMERICA's first supersalesmen were Yankee peddlers from Connecticut. They traveled all over the country, their wagons loaded with goods for the homes of pioneer America. Many Connecticut towns still manufacture the same products they made in the early days of our nation. Waterbury is famous for its clocks and brassware, Meriden for its silverware, Willimantic for its thread and Danbury for its hats.

It was native Connecticut know-how that created the wide variety of made-in-Connecticut goods. Here Yale invented his lock and John Howe developed a machine to make pins; Singer and Wilson invented their sewing machine and Colt perfected his revolver.

Connecticut was the Pequot Indian word for the *Long River*. The Connecticut River is the longest river in New England. In the valley through which it flows, the farmers of Connecticut raise tobacco, potatoes, fruit and vegetables.

On Long Island Sound—where the "Long River" empties —are Connecticut's busy port cities: Bridgeport, New Haven and New London. New London is also home for the U.S. Coast Guard Academy. And across the river at Groton Naval Base the first atomic-powered submarine—the *Nautilus*—was launched.

If you had lived in Abington in 1793, you might have read books from what is now the oldest lending library in the U.S. If you had gone to school at East Haddam in 1774, your teacher might have been—Nathan Hale!

DELAWARE

"The Diamond State" became the 1st State, 1787

 "I SEE a white, sandy shore and an abundance of green trees," Henry Hudson wrote in 1609, as he sailed up the Delaware River.

Imagine that you are taking Hudson for a trip through Delaware today. Instead of trees, Hudson sees abundant smokestacks. For factories are an important part of the city of Wilmington, the state's largest city.

As he sails down the Delaware again, Hudson sees great ocean liners and busy freighters. Piled high on the docks are crates and cartons to be loaded aboard waiting ships.

"These crates hold machinery and ammunition," you say. "And chemicals, dyes and leather goods. So many chemicals are made here that Wilmington is called the Chemical Capital of the World. And over here are cartons marked 'Nylon.' That's a cloth spun out of coal, air and water."

"Nylon!" exclaims Hudson. "'Tis more like witchcraft. Does witchcraft make all these wonders?"

"No," you explain. "These goods are made by people."

Hudson holds up a crate of eggs. "These, too?"

You assure him that eggs still come from chickens and that Delaware farms raise millions of them. Then you show him fields of berries, corn, wheat and tomatoes.

Finally you take Henry Hudson to Delaware Bay. You point out the oyster boats with their great derrick-like dredges. "These scoop up the oysters," you say. This is too much! With a deep sigh, the old ghost vanishes from the sandy shores of the state he explored long ago.

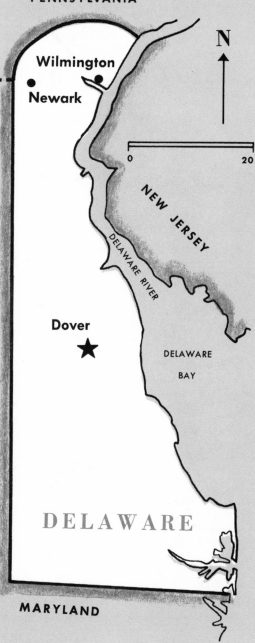

PENNSYLVANIA

Wilmington

Newark

N

0   20

NEW JERSEY

DELAWARE RIVER

Dover

★

DELAWARE BAY

DELAWARE

MARYLAND

• Delaware has a special honor. Because it was the first of the thirteen original states to sign the Constitution, Delaware leads the parade of states every four years when the new President is inaugurated.

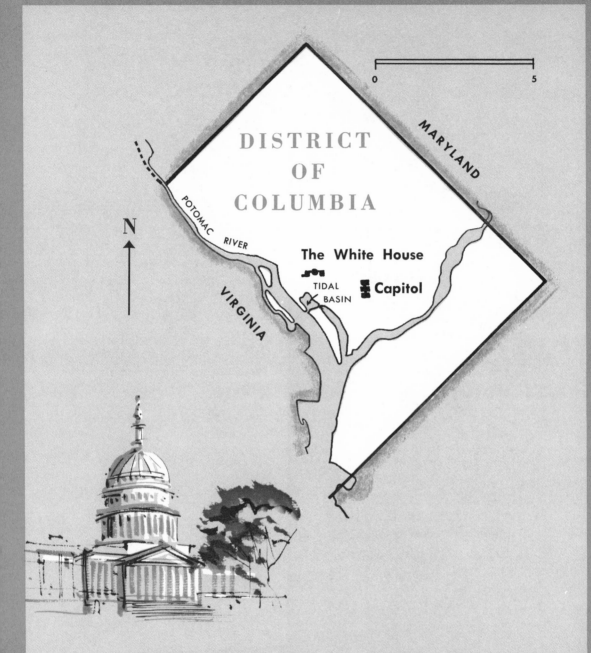

DISTRICT
OF
COLUMBIA

MARYLAND

POTOMAC RIVER

N

VIRGINIA

The White House

TIDAL BASIN

Capitol

0   5

• All major streets in Washington lead to the Capitol building like spokes in a wheel. Here Congress meets to make our country's laws. George Washington laid the cornerstone of the Capitol in 1793. The inauguration of U.S. presidents usually takes place on the steps of the Capitol.

DISTRICT OF COLUMBIA

 WHICH city is the capital of all our states but isn't a part of any state? Washington, D.C., of course, which became our capital in 1800.

Our first President worked hard to see our capital city built. He chose the site—the banks of the Potomac River. But George Washington never lived in his namesake city. John Adams was the first tenant of the White House, which has been the home of our presidents ever since.

Government is Washington's main business. Here Congress meets to make our laws. Here the highest court in our land convenes—the Supreme Court. One of every three people in Washington works for the U.S. government. There's plenty of work to be done, too! Here in Washington are the busy "main offices" of government departments such as the Treasury and Agriculture.

The Bureau of Engraving and Printing makes our paper money and stamps. The Library of Congress is one of the world's largest libraries. In the National Archives building, you can see two thrilling original documents—the Declaration of Independence and the Constitution.

Washington is one of the loveliest capitals in the world. It's a city of wide avenues (named for different states), green parks, white marble buildings and impressive memorials, such as the Jefferson and Lincoln memorials. In the spring Washington is especially beautiful. Then 3,000 Japanese cherry trees along the Tidal Basin burst into bloom—a breath-taking sight.

FLORIDA

"The Sunshine State" became the 27th State, 1845

WHERE do circuses go in the winter? To Sarasota, Florida. Besides circuses in the winter, Florida has hogs that fish, cows that dunk—and pink birds. On Lake George, near Seville, the hogs swim out in the shallow water to catch their fish dinners. The bottom of the lake is covered with thick grass so cows must duck their heads underwater to reach their food. And the pink flamingos of Hialeah Park eat only with their heads upside down!

Florida has about 30,000 lakes—more than any other state. It also has the longest highway ever built over ocean waters. The Overseas Highway runs from Miami to Key West, spanning the islands called the Florida Keys, at the end of the peninsula of Florida.

Florida tans are famous. Northern visitors acquire them at Florida's sandy beaches and winter resorts.

Florida's jungles are famous, too. In the swampy Everglades deer and panthers roam, and alligators sun themselves.

Where can you eat grapefruit and oranges right from the trees? In Florida, where vegetables and sugar cane are also raised. From Florida's forests comes our main supply of cypress lumber. And from its pine trees comes much of our turpentine. There's cigar making at Tampa, and sponge fishing at nearby Tarpon Springs.

What is the oldest town in the U.S.? St. Augustine, Florida, the first permanent European settlement in the U.S., founded about 1565.

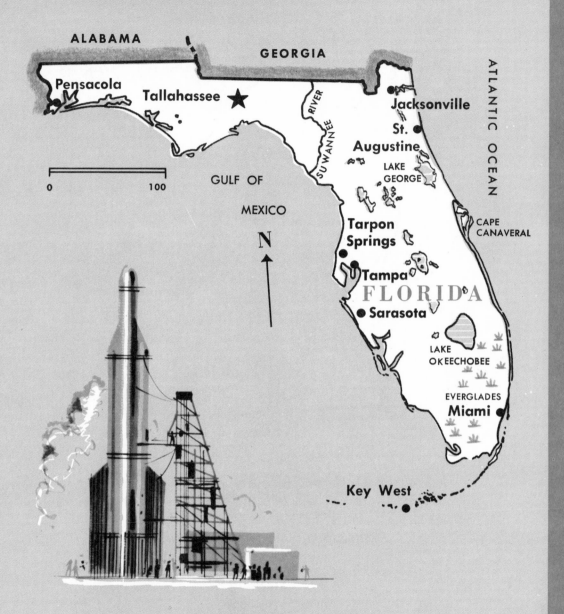

ALABAMA

GEORGIA

Pensacola

Tallahassee ★

ATLANTIC OCEAN

Jacksonville

St.
Augustine

LAKE
GEORGE

GULF OF

MEXICO

SUWANNEE RIVER

0   100

N

CAPE
CANAVERAL

Tarpon
Springs

Tampa

FLORIDA

Sarasota

LAKE
OKEECHOBEE

EVERGLADES
Miami

Key West

• The John F. Kennedy Space Center is located at Florida's Cape Canaveral. From the cape's launching platforms, huge rockets thunder into space. *Explorer I*, America's first earth satellite, was launched from Canaveral. So were our first astronauts.

TENNESSEE   NORTH CAROLINA

ALABAMA

★ Atlanta

● Warm Springs

● Columbus

N

GEORGIA

SAVANNAH RIVER

SOUTH CAROLINA

Savannah ●

SEA ISLANDS

ATLANTIC OCEAN

OKEFENOKEE SWAMP

FLORIDA

0   100

• Franklin D. Roosevelt, thirty-second President of the U.S., was stricken with polio at the age of 39. Treatment and swimming at Warm Springs helped him to regain much of his strength. To help other polio sufferers, he started the Warm Springs Foundation.

GEORGIA

"Empire State of the South" became the 4th State, 1788

 THE climate was perfect for raising cotton. Georgia's farmers knew it. But few of them wanted the weary job of separating cotton fiber from its seed. Then in 1793, in Savannah, Eli Whitney invented his cotton gin—a mechanical wonder that could clean the seeds from 350 pounds of cotton in one day! Cotton became king in Georgia —its main crop for many years. And soon there were textile mills busily turning the cotton into cloth.

Georgia is the third largest producer of cotton goods in the U.S. Now its farmers grow a variety of crops that includes pecans, watermelons, sugar, Georgia's famous peaches —and peanuts! More peanuts are grown in Georgia than in any other state.

The newsprint for some of your newspapers and the plastics for some of your games may have begun life in the pine forests which cover two-thirds of Georgia. From Georgia's quarries came the marble stone for the beautiful Lincoln Memorial in Washington, D.C.

Georgia is the largest state east of the Mississippi River. With a coastline almost 100 miles long and Appalachian peaks rising in the north, its scenery is richly varied. Just off the shore are the famous Sea Islands. And in the south is vast eerie Okefenokee Swamp, "the place of trembling earth," where floating islands of tangled weeds tremble under the slightest weight. Okefenokee is one of the largest swamps in the U.S. Much of Okefenokee is still a mysterious place that has never been explored.

HAWAII

"The Aloha State" became the 50th State, 1959

THE HAWAIIAN word *aloha* means several things— *welcome, good-by, love,* and *friendship.* It also describes the way people from many parts of the world live together on these beautiful islands in peace and friendship. A Hawaiian child may have ancestors from Japan, China, Europe, North America, or the Philippines.

Our newest state is our only island state. It is really a chain of 20 islands, formed by the tops of undersea mountains. Most of these are so small they are just dots on a map. People live only on the seven largest islands.

Oahu is the most important island because of Honolulu, Hawaii's capital, biggest port, and only large city. Here, too, is our great naval base, Pearl Harbor.

Hawaii grows more sugar cane than any other state, and much of it comes from Kauai, the "Garden Island." Near Kauai's highest point is Mount Waialeale, one of the world's rainiest places.

Lanai is a big pineapple plantation. From the Hawaiian Islands come most of the world's canned pineapple products.

On Maui there is an immense sleeping volcano. Once, in a fiery explosion, it blew its top off. The hole that was left is the world's largest inactive-volcano crater.

The giant volcanoes of Mauna Kea and Mauna Loa rise over "Big Island," Hawaii, which has the same name as the state. Here you can see cowboys herding cattle on big ranches.

Hawaiians greet their thousands of visitors with garlands of flowers called *leis,* and the friendly cry *"Aloha!"*

KAUAI

NIIHAU

PACIFIC OCEAN

N

OAHU

Honolulu

MOLOKAI

MAUI

HAWAII

LANAI

KAHOOLAWE

0   100

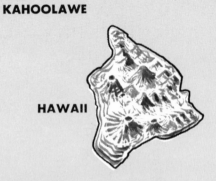

HAWAII

• Surfboard riding over the waves is a popular sport among Hawaiian children and grownups. It was invented long ago by the kings and chieftains of Hawaii. Surfboarding requires skill and courage but it comes easily to our island-dwelling citizens.

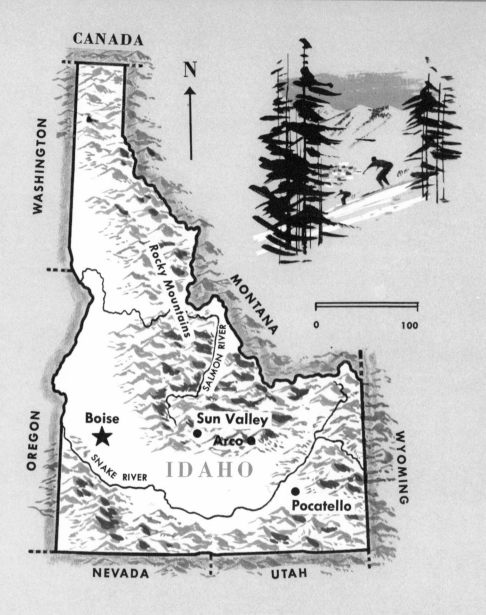

• Vacationers from all over the world come to Sun Valley's famous sports resort. During the winter visitors can enjoy skiing on Sun Valley's twenty ski runs. In the summer tourists can hunt, fish or go mountain climbing. Sun Valley is 6,000 feet above sea level and is encircled by snowy peaks.

IDAHO

"The Gem State" became the 43rd State, 1890

 IF you woke up one morning in a park near Sun Valley called Craters of the Moon, you might think you *were* on the moon. You would see brightly colored lava fields and the dead craters of extinct volcanoes.

Other things in Idaho seem to come out of science fiction, too. There are caves whose walls are thick with ice that never melts. Other caves contain springs so hot that the water is piped out to heat homes.

In the Snake River live giant white sturgeon, the biggest fresh-water fish in North America. Some weigh more than a thousand pounds. In order to pull out a big one, fishermen have been known to hitch their lines to a two-horse wagon.

Most people in Idaho live on or near the banks of the Snake. From this river's surging waters comes their electrical power. The Snake is certainly not "small potatoes"!

In fact, Idaho boasts that it doesn't have any small potatoes —only the big Idaho potatoes that grow in the farmlands of the Snake River plains.

The jagged mountains of Idaho's Rockies are as fierce as their names—Sawtooth, Seven Devils, Bitterroot. There are riches in the Idaho mountains—gold and zinc, antimony, cobalt and lead, and semi-precious stones. The largest silver mines in the U.S. are in Idaho, too.

Near the edge of the mountains not far from Sun Valley is an important center for atomic research. Here, at Arco, the first electricity ever to come from atomic energy was produced in 1951.

ILLINOIS

"The Prairie State" became the 21st State, 1818

 DOWN the Illinois River the early settlers sailed. Down the Ohio, the Wabash and the Mississippi, too. They came to Illinois by keelboat and barge, and they came overland by wagon.

Some came to farm the fertile meadows. And as Illinois farmers do even today, they raised corn, hogs and cattle and shipped them to market down their river highways. Some came to build and work in towns. Thus the cities of Rockford, Decatur, Joliet and Evanston grew. Still others came to mine the coal needed for the growing factories. Today these factories produce the most farm machinery, candy, and corn products in the nation.

In the 1770's, a successful Negro fur trader established a trading post on the north bank of the Chicago River. He was Jean Baptiste Point du Sable and his trading post was the beginning of a mighty city—Chicago!

Today Chicago leads the world as a railway center and as a grain and livestock market. It's our largest lake port, and second only to New York City in printing and publishing.

Chicago and its neighbor cities produce more steel than Pittsburgh. Raw materials, such as the iron ore from mines near Lake Superior, are transported easily and cheaply to the foundries and steel mills of Chicago and its suburbs and, just across the state line, to Gary, Indiana.

In 1871 the Great Chicago Fire destroyed almost the entire city. What started the fire? An overturned kerosene lamp. Who started the fire? Mrs. O'Leary's cow, they say.

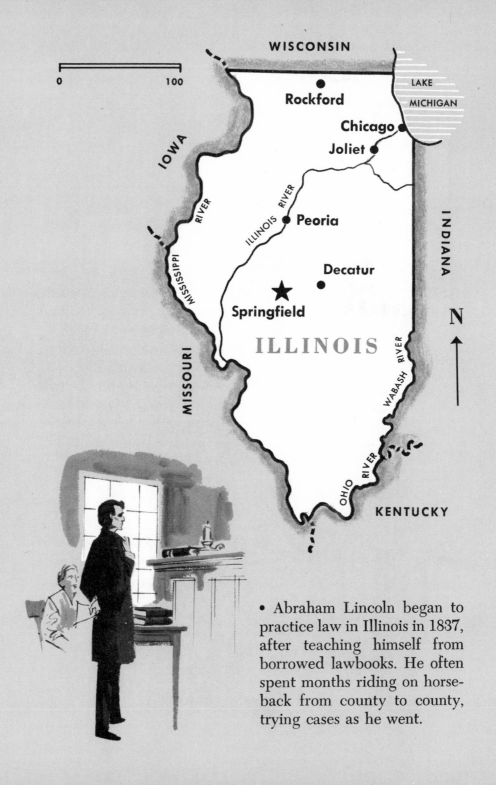

WISCONSIN

IOWA

0   100

Rockford

LAKE
MICHIGAN

Chicago

Joliet

ILLINOIS RIVER

Peoria

INDIANA

MISSISSIPPI RIVER

Decatur

N

Springfield

ILLINOIS

WABASH RIVER

OHIO RIVER

MISSOURI

KENTUCKY

• Abraham Lincoln began to practice law in Illinois in 1837, after teaching himself from borrowed lawbooks. He often spent months riding on horseback from county to county, trying cases as he went.

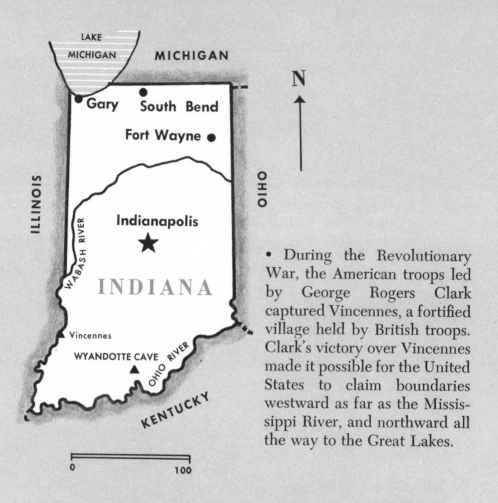

LAKE
MICHIGAN

MICHIGAN

• Gary   South Bend

Fort Wayne •

ILLINOIS

OHIO

WABASH RIVER

Indianapolis

★

INDIANA

Vincennes

WYANDOTTE CAVE ▲

OHIO RIVER

KENTUCKY

N
↑

0   100

• During the Revolutionary War, the American troops led by George Rogers Clark captured Vincennes, a fortified village held by British troops. Clark's victory over Vincennes made it possible for the United States to claim boundaries westward as far as the Mississippi River, and northward all the way to the Great Lakes.

INDIANA

"The Hoosier State" became the 19th State, 1816

SOMETIMES cities grow fast. At first Gary, Indiana, was a small port on the sandy shores of Lake Michigan. But Gary had coal and limestone. With coal and limestone, iron ore can be turned into steel. Minnesota had iron ore to ship to Gary. As the ore poured in, Gary grew like Jack's beanstalk. Today Gary is a bustling city, its giant mills turning out steel night and day!

It is also hard to believe that Indianapolis, the largest city in Indiana, was once two log cabins and an Indian footpath. The people chose Indianapolis for their capital because it was almost in the exact center of the state.

Indiana has farms as well as cities. It is one of the leading states in growing corn, soybeans and tomatoes. On its level plains grow corn, alfalfa and oats, and its fields of wheat stretch like a golden sea. When the corn and grain are cut and stacked, they look like yellow wigwams. Hogs are Indiana's most valuable livestock product, and beef cattle are next in importance.

Real wigwams once dotted the plains of Indiana, for this was the home of the Shawnee and Miami Indians.

Indiana can boast of two most unusual places. One is Wyandotte Cave, one of the largest natural caves in the country. Here narrow passages wind for miles through underground rooms.

The other special place is named Santa Claus. Not for St. Nick, of course. It's the town where most of the letters addressed to Santa find their way.

31

IOWA

"The Hawkeye State" became the 29th State, 1846

 MOST of Iowa is a king-size prairie as flat as the floor in your room. And on this land there's a living carpet of corn, grain and hay. Iowa's farmers raise so many crops it is said that "Iowa feeds the nation."

Iowa has always been good farmland. Before white men came, Indians raised corn, tilling their fields with pointed deerhorns. How astonished these Indians would be if they could see Iowa today! Modern farm machinery, made in Iowa's cities, helps turn the soil and harvest the crops. Hogs and cattle feed on Iowa's golden corn and grain.

The Indians would marvel, too, at the up-to-date meat-packing plants which turn Iowa livestock into pork, beef and mutton. But they would see one familiar sight. In the city of Muscatine there are factories that make pearl buttons from shells of mussels—the same kind of mussel shells the Indians used to make their necklaces and spoons.

Iowans can boast not only of their king-size prairies that grow king-size corn. They also have the *largest* washing machine factory, the *largest* cereal mill and the *largest* popcorn processing plant in the U.S.

One of Iowa's proudest boasts is its leadership in education. No other state has a better record in teaching its people to read and write.

The town of Pella was founded by settlers from the Netherlands in 1847. Now every May, Pella holds a Dutch Tulip Festival. The town dresses up in tulips and the townsfolk dress up in wooden shoes.

32

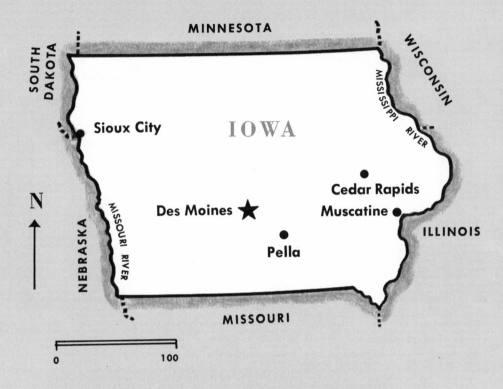

• Iowa has some of the richest soil in the world and takes turns with Illinois in growing the most corn of any state. Some of the corn is made into corn meal and cereal, but most of it goes to feed hogs and cattle.

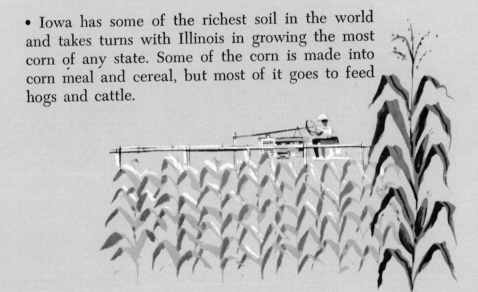

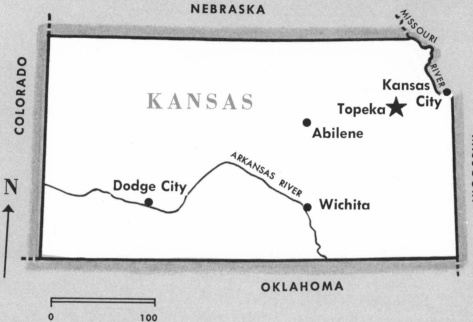

NEBRASKA

COLORADO

MISSOURI RIVER

KANSAS

Kansas City

Topeka

Abilene

N

ARKANSAS RIVER

Dodge City

Wichita

MISSOURI

OKLAHOMA

0   100

• William Frederick Cody got his nickname of "Buffalo Bill" by shooting thousands of buffalo to provide meat for hungry men who built the Kansas Pacific Railroad. Cody had been a Pony Express rider and served as an Army scout. He also organized America's first Wild West show, which featured cowboys and Indians performing daredevil feats of riding, roping and shooting.

KANSAS

"The Sunflower State" became the 34th State, 1861

THE Spanish explorer Coronado came to Kansas in 1541, looking for gold. All he found were small Indian villages and miles and miles of flatland.

The only gold in Kansas today are vast golden fields of wheat and corn edged with the gold of sunflowers. So much winter wheat is grown and so much flour is milled in Kansas that it has been nicknamed the "breadbasket" of the nation.

Much of the wheat goes to Kansas City and Wichita, which have the largest flour mills. Here, too, are stockyards and meat-packing plants, oil fields and airplane factories.

Two pioneer Kansas towns, Abilene and Dodge City, are famous in song and story. In the 1870's, they were wild frontier towns. Weary cowboys drove herds of cattle to market along the Chisholm Trail from Texas to Abilene. On the streets of Dodge City, desperados shot it out with strong-nerved sheriffs and marshals. There, too, Bat Masterson and Wyatt Earp served terms as peace officers.

Kansas towns are no longer wild, but Kansas weather is still untamed. The wind blows and blows and once in a while it blows up into a rip-roaring tornado. (It was a Kansas storm that blew Dorothy to the Land of Oz!)

But once it was known as "Bleeding Kansas." Even before the Civil War began, bloody battles were fought here over slavery. Some wanted Kansas to be a free state. Others wanted to keep slaves. But Kansas remained loyal to the Union, and one-fifth of its men fought against slavery.

KENTUCKY

"The Bluegrass State" became the 15th State, 1792

KENTUCKY was our first state west of the Appalachian Mountains. It took brave men and women to settle this frontier—pioneers like those Daniel Boone led through the Cumberland Gap in 1775. Encircled by hostile Indians, they built their fort, called it Boonesborough—and *stayed*.

So many Indian battles were fought in Kentucky its name is said to mean *dark and bloody ground*. But when the Indian wars were over, the settlers found Kentucky a good place to live in. They liked the mild climate and the fine rich soil.

Today in this fertile soil Kentucky farmers grow the nation's second largest tobacco crop. Once tobacco was the only crop. It was even used instead of money. Now vegetables, fruit and grain also grow here. And grass seed from the farms of Kentucky has sprouted in parks and lawns in many parts of the world. Kentucky's horse farms are famous, too, for the fine race horses they breed.

Kentucky has rich coal deposits and ranks second as a coal-producing state. Oil and gas, clay and limestone, are also taken from the earth. There's gold underground in Kentucky but it won't ever start a gold rush. For this treasure is America's gold reserve, and our government keeps it stored in underground vaults at Fort Knox.

Kentucky has another kind of under-the-earth "treasure" in Mammoth Cave. Imagine a cave with rooms high enough to hold a twelve-story building, with lakes and waterfalls and rushing rivers—a vast underground world!

36

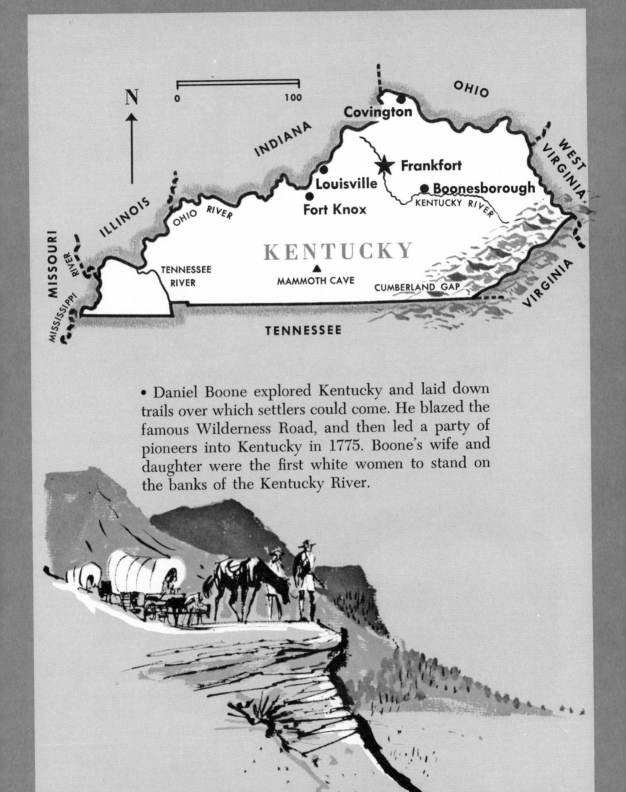

• Daniel Boone explored Kentucky and laid down trails over which settlers could come. He blazed the famous Wilderness Road, and then led a party of pioneers into Kentucky in 1775. Boone's wife and daughter were the first white women to stand on the banks of the Kentucky River.

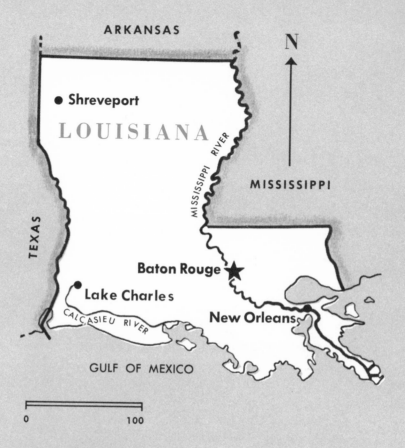

ARKANSAS

N

● Shreveport

LOUISIANA

MISSISSIPPI RIVER

MISSISSIPPI

TEXAS

Baton Rouge ★

● Lake Charles

CALCASIEU RIVER

New Orleans

GULF OF MEXICO

0   100

• New Orleans' Mardi Gras carnival takes place every year several weeks before Easter. This festival was introduced in New Orleans by the French colonists about 1857. During Mardi Gras, parades, floats and masks bob up everywhere. The name *Mardi Gras* means *fat Tuesday* in French—a time of feasting and fun.

LOUISIANA

"The Pelican State" became the 18th State, 1812

FROM frogs to fish, Louisiana is a land of "mosts." It grows more sugar cane than any state but Hawaii. More muskrats are trapped in its swamps and bayous than in Canada and our other states combined. One of the biggest catches of fresh fish is taken by Louisiana fishermen from the Gulf of Mexico. Yes, there *are* more frogs in Louisiana than in any other state. And the greatest variety of game birds in the U.S. can be found here, many of them living in the large sanctuaries where wildlife is protected.

Louisiana's main cities are deep-water ports—New Orleans, Lake Charles and the capital city of Baton Rouge. The state's largest city is New Orleans, one of the nation's major ports. About a hundred years ago steamboats carried goods and passengers up the Mississippi to St. Louis in Missouri. Today ships sail from New Orleans with cotton, sugar, and oil for ports in both nearby and faraway lands.

The United States government bought the Louisiana Territory from France in 1803 for fifteen million dollars. Louisiana was one of the thirteen new states—or parts of states—that were formed from this territory.

The French influence is still so strong that New Orleans has been called the "Paris of America," and the Old French Quarter in the city—the Vieux Carré—is known for its restaurants and shops. New Orleans is also famous for the gayest festival in the South—the Mardi Gras. People wear wonderful costumes and hold colorful parades and pageants. Even the lampposts of New Orleans dress up for the Mardi Gras!

MAINE

"The Pine Tree State" became the 23rd State, 1820

WHERE does the sun rise first in the U.S.? In Eastport, Maine—most easterly city in America.

Where do Florida fish go for their vacation? Some end up in Maine's Kennebec River. Great tides from the Atlantic Ocean sweep into the Kennebec, bringing in all kinds of fish from the sea.

The lumbering industry of America was born in Maine. In colonial days, when Maine was a part of the Massachusetts Bay Colony, the British Navy ordered all Maine pines over two feet thick to be marked "Reserved." These great trees became the booms and masts of England's sailing ships.

The first ship in America was built in Maine, and ship-building continued to be an important industry for years. Today trees of Maine provide the pulp out of which paper is made in Maine's paper mills. Its factories also turn out shoes and textiles.

Many a mouth-watering meal travels to your dinner table from Maine. Big lobsters, potatoes and blueberry pie, for example! Maine catches three-fourths of the nation's lobsters. It grows more potatoes than any other state except Idaho and much of the nation's blueberries.

Would you like to explore the green forests of our largest New England state? Or paddle in a canoe down its rivers and streams? Or see Maine's highest mountain—Mount Katahdin? You won't find a better guide than one of Maine's own Indians. They are very much in demand, for Maine and vacations go together like ham and eggs.

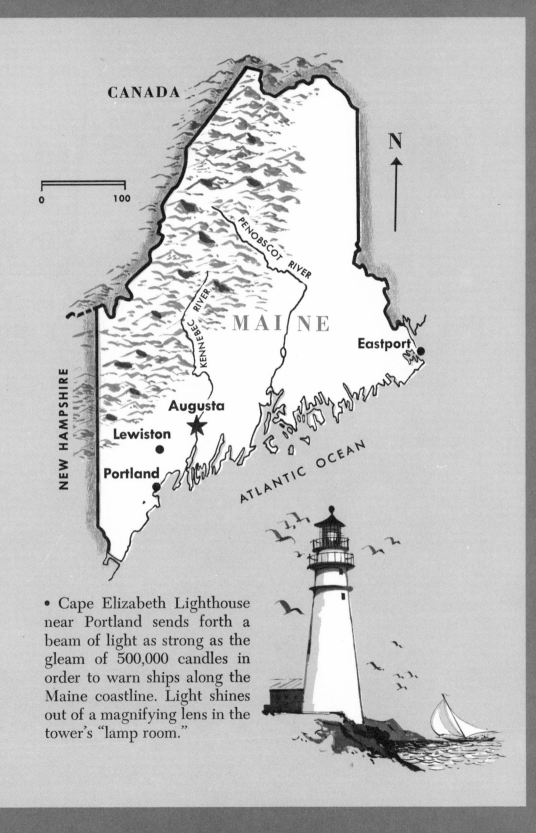

CANADA

N

0   100

PENOBSCOT RIVER

KENNEBEC RIVER

MAINE

Eastport

NEW HAMPSHIRE

Augusta

Lewiston

Portland

ATLANTIC OCEAN

• Cape Elizabeth Lighthouse near Portland sends forth a beam of light as strong as the gleam of 500,000 candles in order to warn ships along the Maine coastline. Light shines out of a magnifying lens in the tower's "lamp room."

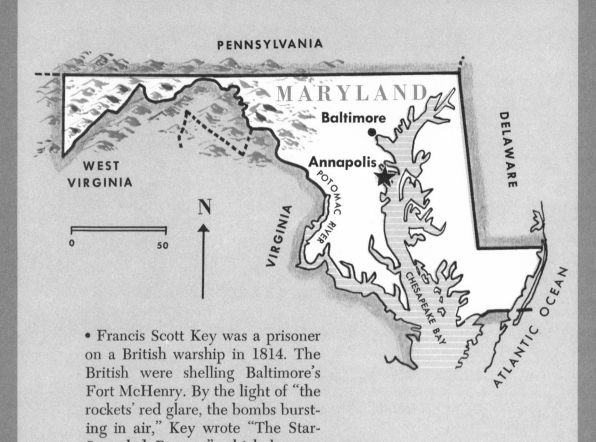

PENNSYLVANIA

MARYLAND

WEST VIRGINIA

Baltimore

Annapolis

DELAWARE

VIRGINIA

POTOMAC RIVER

CHESAPEAKE BAY

ATLANTIC OCEAN

N

0   50

• Francis Scott Key was a prisoner on a British warship in 1814. The British were shelling Baltimore's Fort McHenry. By the light of "the rockets' red glare, the bombs bursting in air," Key wrote "The Star-Spangled Banner," which became our national anthem.

MARYLAND

"The Old Line State" became the 7th State, 1788

 MARYLAND has an open doorway to the sea—Chesapeake Bay. On the map, the Bay looks like a ragged tear that divides Maryland in two.

From Chesapeake Bay and its jagged inlets, Maryland fishermen haul in millions of pounds of fish, oysters, crabs and clams each year. On the Eastern Shore are truck farms where corn, wheat, strawberries and tomatoes are raised. Maryland's fruit and vegetable crop is canned or frozen on the Eastern Shore or sent fresh to large eastern cities.

Because Chesapeake Bay is big and deep enough for ocean-going ships, Baltimore is a great port city. In colonial days, it was the furthest inland of all U.S. ports and a gateway to the West. The rich coal fields of Maryland's neighbor states made Baltimore a great coal-shipping center. Today the steel and shipbuilding plants make Baltimore a major industrial city as well.

Maryland's capital, Annapolis, was once the capital of the U.S. From 1783 to 1784 Congress met in the State House. Annapolis is also the home of the U.S. Naval Academy. In the chapel of the Academy lies the body of America's first great naval hero—John Paul Jones.

The next time you travel on a train, think of Maryland, where the first passenger-carrying American railway was born. Maryland saw another important beginning, too. In 1844, in Washington, D.C., Samuel F. B. Morse tapped out a message on his new invention. To Baltimore came those historic first words ever sent by telegraph: WHAT HATH GOD WROUGHT?

MASSACHUSETTS

"The Bay State" became the 6th State, 1788

WALKING in and around Boston is like strolling through American history. You are not far from the very ground where the Battle of Bunker Hill was fought. In the Old State House, you see a bottle of tea that came from the Boston Tea Party. And you look up at the belfry of the Old North Church half expecting to see the two lanterns that told Paul Revere the British were coming by sea.

The first library, the first newspaper, the first public school, the first college in America—they all began in Massachusetts. And in 1621, the Pilgrims celebrated the first Thanksgiving.

The cranberries you eat at your Thanksgiving dinner probably still come from Massachusetts. Cranberries are one of this state's most important crops.

Today in Massachusetts the valley of the Connecticut River yields harvests of hay, tobacco and vegetables. But the first colonists had a hard time raising crops on the stony ground where they settled. Later they turned to manufacturing. The first woolen mill and iron works were built in Massachusetts. Today a huge electrical machinery and electronics industry is centered in the Boston area.

Back in the 1800's Massachusetts boys seeking adventure signed up on the whaling boats that sailed out of New Bedford, Salem and Nantucket. Whale-hunting was a big business then. So was the building of Boston's fast "Yankee Clipper" sailing ships. The clipper ships are gone, but there are still wind-filled sails in the coves and bays of Massachusetts. For in this state sailing is a favorite sport.

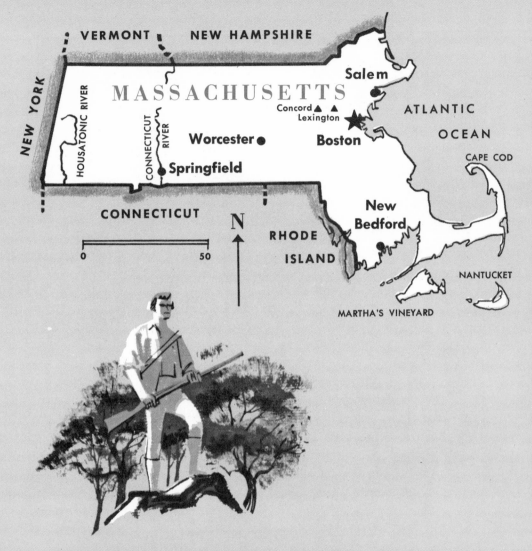

VERMONT NEW HAMPSHIRE

NEW YORK

MASSACHUSETTS

HOUSATONIC RIVER

CONNECTICUT RIVER

Salem

Concord ▲ ▲
Lexington

★

Worcester ●

Boston

Springfield ●

ATLANTIC

OCEAN

CAPE COD

CONNECTICUT

N

RHODE
ISLAND

New
Bedford ●

NANTUCKET

0   50

MARTHA'S VINEYARD

• This statue of a Minuteman stands in Concord. It is dedicated to the memory of the men who volunteered to bear arms "at a minute's notice" to defend their country during the Revolutionary War. Massachusetts Minutemen fought bravely against British troops in the battles of Concord and Lexington. The "shot heard round the world," which began the war, was fired at Lexington on April 19, 1775.

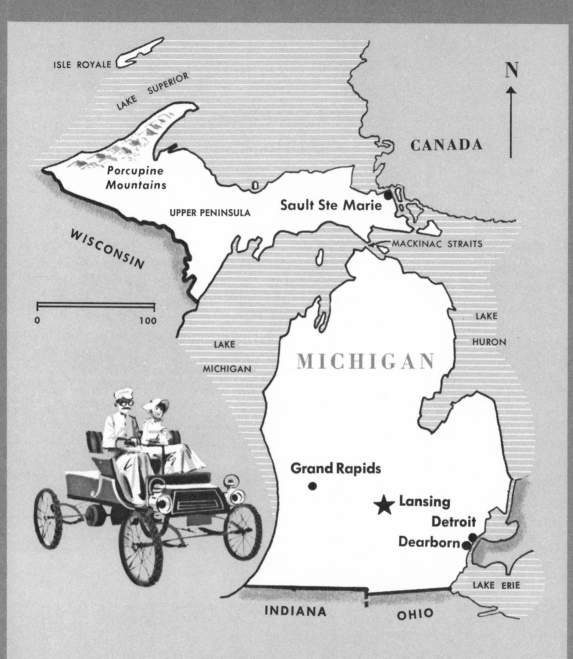

N

ISLE ROYALE

LAKE SUPERIOR

CANADA

Porcupine
Mountains

UPPER PENINSULA

Sault Ste Marie

WISCONSIN

MACKINAC STRAITS

0   100

LAKE
HURON

LAKE
MICHIGAN

MICHIGAN

Grand Rapids

Lansing

Detroit

Dearborn

LAKE ERIE

INDIANA   OHIO

• It was in Detroit that cars were first produced on
an assembly line. Henry Ford speeded up car production by adding conveyor belts to assembly lines.
This cut the time it took to make a car from 14 hours
to 93 minutes. Today cars are produced in about an
hour. The car pictured above is an early Rambler.

MICHIGAN

"The Wolverine State" became the 26th State, 1837

DETROIT, Michigan's largest city, has been called the world's Car Capital. More autos are made in and around Detroit than in any other place. And although it is 1,600 miles from the ocean, Detroit is one of the nation's largest ports. Thanks to the St. Lawrence Seaway, ocean vessels can now sail from the Atlantic to the Great Lakes—right to the docks of Detroit.

Michigan is the only state whose shores are washed by four of the five Great Lakes—Erie, Huron, Michigan and Superior. There's almost as much traffic on Michigan's waterways as there is on its city streets. The Sault Sainte Marie Canal carries more freight than any other canal in the world. Barges sail through the canal, bringing iron ore from Minnesota. The ore is for Michigan's mills to make into steel. The steel is for Michigan's auto plants to make into cars.

The Mackinac Straits divide Michigan in two. In the Upper Peninsula are green pine woods and the Porcupine Mountains. If you live in the Lower Peninsula, your home may be on a farm or in one of the busy factory cities of Dearborn, Detroit or Lansing, the capital. The Mackinac Bridge, across the straits, is one of the world's longest suspension bridges.

In the modern city of Dearborn there's an historic village —Greenfield Village, built by Henry Ford, pioneer builder of automobiles. Here you can go right back into yesterday and see an old mill, a cigar-store Indian, a riverboat—even a reproduction of Thomas Edison's first laboratory.

MINNESOTA

"The Gopher State" became the 32nd State, 1858

MILLIONS of years ago in Minnesota, great glaciers moved across the land. Ridges were pushed up to form the Vermilion, Cuyuna and Mesabi Ranges. Earth was flattened, making the fine plains where wheat and corn now grow. Thousands of hollows were scooped out by the glaciers, and as these glaciers melted, the hollows filled with water to become Minnesota's sky-blue lakes.

The port city of Duluth is on the largest of these lakes— Lake Superior. Iron ore is loaded onto cargo boats and shipped from Duluth to the great steel mills.

Minnesota produces most of our iron ore. The largest man-made hole in the world is the open-pit mine at Hibbing, where iron ore is so close to the surface of the ground it can be scooped up by steam shovels.

With so much iron ore in Minnesota, you'd think mining was the largest industry. Yet Minnesota is chiefly a farming state—often called our "Bread and Butter" state. Vast quantities of flour used for making bread are milled in Minnesota's towns, and only Wisconsin produces more butter.

Minnesota has its own tale of two cities. These are the twin cities that face each other on opposite sides of the Mississippi —St. Paul, capital of the state, and Minneapolis, its largest city.

Some like it hot. Some like it cold. In Minnesota you're lucky if you like both. For in winter the temperature may dip to 40 degrees below zero—and in summer it may zoom to 100 degrees.

48

CANADA

INTERNATIONAL FALLS

NORTH DAKOTA

Hibbing

Duluth

LAKE SUPERIOR

MINNESOTA

MISSISSIPPI RIVER

SOUTH DAKOTA

0   100

N

WISCONSIN

Minneapolis

St. Paul

Rochester

IOWA

• Paul Bunyan is a favorite hero of American folklore. He was a giant lumberjack, "as strong as a hundred men." His friend and companion was Babe—the immense Blue Ox, who drank rivers dry. These statues stand by Lake Bemidji.

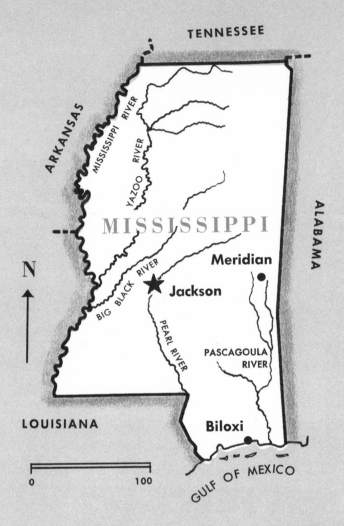

TENNESSEE

ARKANSAS

MISSISSIPPI RIVER

YAZOO RIVER

MISSISSIPPI

ALABAMA

N

BIG BLACK RIVER

Meridian

Jackson

PEARL RIVER

PASCAGOULA RIVER

LOUISIANA

Biloxi

0   100

GULF OF MEXICO

• Captains of steamboats on the
Mississippi River were proud of
their vessels' speed, and often
held races. In the last and
most famous race, in
1870, the *Robert E. Lee*
beat the *Natchez* from
New Orleans to St. Louis.

MISSISSIPPI

"The Magnolia State" became the 20th State, 1817

MISSISSIPPI is a land of farms. The mild climate and rich black soil make it easy to raise peanuts, soybeans, sugar, corn and rice. And cotton, of course! This warm, sunny state ranks third as a cotton producer. The dairy farmers of Mississippi are busy too. They feed and milk more than two million cows every day.

Mississippi sends what it produces far and wide. How do its goods travel? Down the greatest river highway in the land—the Mississippi River. From the wharves of any Mississippi river town, you can see cargoes of corn and cotton being loaded onto boats and barges.

Lumber is an important cargo, too, for Mississippi is a land of forests as well as rivers. Forests cover more than half of the state. Cutting down trees is one way of earning a living here. Working in the sawmills that turn logs into lumber is another. Today oil production is important in Mississippi.

When the river rises higher than its banks, the friendly Mississippi becomes an enemy. Artificial riverbanks called levees have been built to keep the rising waters from washing away homes and farms.

Other long rivers with musical names wind through the Magnolia State. Stretching out like two arms from the Mississippi River flow the Big Black and Yazoo Rivers. Off to the Gulf of Mexico wander the waters of the Pascagoula and the Pearl Rivers. A boat trip down the Pearl will take you past cypress swamps, bayous and Jackson, Mississippi's capital and largest city.

51

MISSOURI

"The Show Me State" became the 24th State, 1821

"WANTED—young, skinny, wiry fellows not over 18. Must be expert riders, willing to risk death daily. Orphans preferred. Wages $25 a week."
This ad appeared in a Missouri newspaper in 1860. The daring boys who got the jobs became riders for the Pony Express. They carried the mail from St. Joseph, Missouri, to San Francisco, California, riding through howling snowstorms and burning deserts. Indians chased them and bandits shot at them. But the Pony Express riders got the mail through in ten days.

St. Louis, Missouri's largest city, was once a small trading post for fur trappers. Today this great port on the Mississippi River is a city of skyscrapers and bustling wharves. Beverages, chemicals, drugs and shoes are produced in its factories. Missouri's second largest city, Kansas City, is a great livestock and wheat market.

North of the Missouri River and in the southeast, the soil is fertile and black, yielding a rich harvest of cotton, corn and wheat. So varied are Missouri's resources that this state also mines more lead and raises more mules than any other.

The Ozark Mountains of southern Missouri are rich in springs and caves to explore. The Indians believed these caves were doorways to a life after death.

Which state lies halfway between the Atlantic and the Rocky Mountains? And halfway between Canada and the Gulf of Mexico? Missouri—crossroads of the continental United States.

IOWA

NEBRASKA

ILLINOIS

● St. Joseph

Hannibal ●

MISSOURI RIVER

Kansas City

N

KANSAS

Jefferson City ★

St. Louis

MISSISSIPPI RIVER

MISSOURI

OKLAHOMA

Ozark Mountains

K Y.

ARKANSAS

TENN.

0   100

● This statue of Tom Sawyer and Huck Finn stands in Hannibal, a monument to the adventurous boys author Mark Twain wrote about. Twain's boyhood home in Hannibal is now a museum. Beside the house stands a fence like the one Tom Sawyer tricked his friends into whitewashing for him.

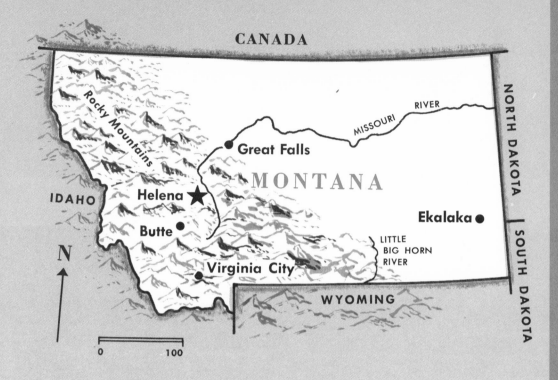

• Montana's forests cover more than 22 million acres, about one-fourth of the state. U.S. Forest Rangers keep a sky-high lookout for dangerous forest fires by patrolling the area in helicopters.

MONTANA

"The Treasure State" became the 41st State, 1889

LESS than a hundred years ago, Montana was the Wild West. Great buffalo herds grazed the plains. Prospectors panned eagerly for gold at Last Chance Gulch and Virginia City. Indians and white men fought for the land, and at Little Big Horn River, General Custer and his men were killed by Sioux and Cheyenne warriors.

How much has Montana changed? Cattle, sheep and horses graze where buffalo once roamed. Great fields of wheat and barely grow where Indians and white men fought. Last Chance Gulch became the state capital, Helena. Virginia City has been rebuilt as a typical town of the old wild West. And a monument marks the lonely spot where Custer died.

In our fourth largest state, mountains cover one-third of the land. Cradled in the northern ridges of the Rocky Mountains lies Glacier National Park. Its 200 lakes are as blue as the sapphires dug from Montana's hillsides. Montana is the only state where sapphires are mined.

The city of Butte is the world's largest "mining camp." Beneath Butte lies another city of mine tunnels and shafts. Here miners dig out millions of dollars' worth of copper, zinc, gold and silver.

Eighty million years ago, prehistoric monsters roamed through Montana. So many dinosaur bones have been found near the town of Ekalaka that ranchers use them for doorstops! No wonder Ekalaka is called Skeleton Flats, or Fossiltown, U.S.A.

NEBRASKA

"The Cornhusker State" became the 37th State, 1867

YOU can still see rutted wheel tracks along Nebraska's Platte and Little Blue Rivers. They were made by the wagons of the pioneers who followed the Platte River Valley westward on their way to Oregon and California in the 1800's. Some of them stopped when they came to Nebraska. They looked around at the grassy plains stretching, it seemed, to the sky. And they liked what they saw—good land to grow their crops. Only trees were missing. So the pioneers planted saplings around their cabins. Today two million acres of Nebraska land are covered with trees.

Most of Nebraska is farmland, and the farmers grow bumper crops of wheat, corn and rye. In the west are Nebraska's vast ranches. Only Texas and Iowa raise more beef cattle.

There are only two large cities in Nebraska, the capital, Lincoln, named for President Lincoln, and Omaha, the major railroad center. The meat-packing industry of Omaha is one of the most important in the world. Omaha was only a camping ground in the wilderness when, in 1804, the two great explorers of the Northwest, Lewis and Clark, camped there with their Indian guides.

Long, long before Lewis and Clark paddled their boats down the Missouri River, Nebraska was explored by quite another kind of "pioneer." These were great 14-foot woolly mammoths, the ancient ancestors of elephants. You can see their fossil remains in the University of Nebraska State Museum in Lincoln.

56

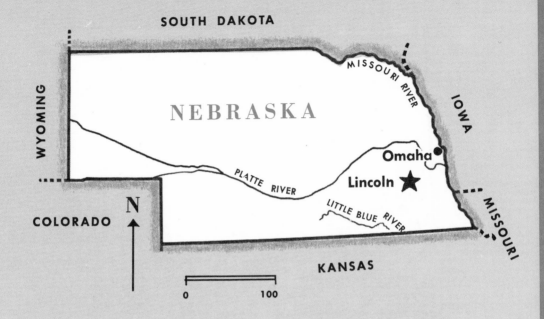

SOUTH DAKOTA

WYOMING

NEBRASKA

MISSOURI RIVER

IOWA

Omaha

Lincoln ★

PLATTE RIVER

LITTLE BLUE RIVER

MISSOURI

N

COLORADO

KANSAS

0   100

• Early Nebraska pioneers found their home a
treeless prairie. They sent back east for young trees
to plant. In 1872 pioneer J. S. Morton set aside
Arbor Day as a special day for planting trees in
Nebraska. Now Arbor Day is celebrated every year
in all the states.

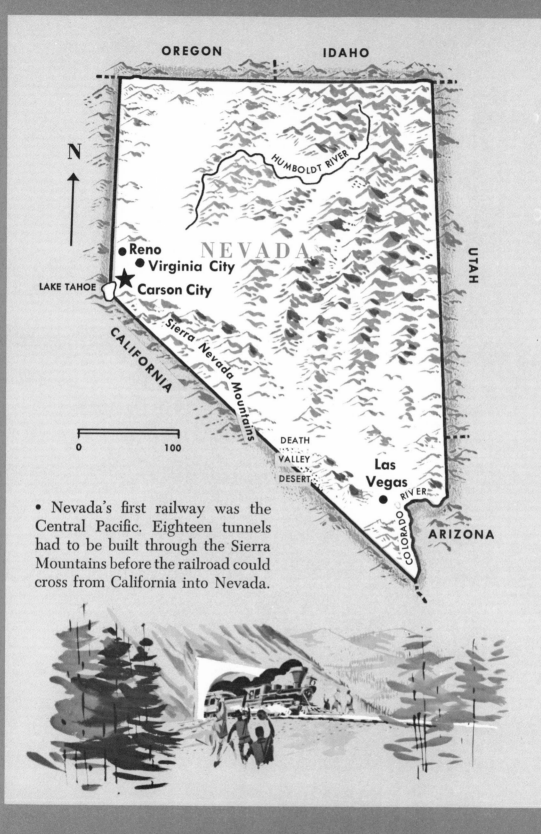

OREGON   IDAHO

N

HUMBOLDT RIVER

NEVADA

● Reno
● Virginia City
★ Carson City

LAKE TAHOE

CALIFORNIA

Sierra Nevada Mountains

UTAH

0   100

DEATH
VALLEY
DESERT

Las
Vegas
●

COLORADO RIVER

ARIZONA

• Nevada's first railway was the
Central Pacific. Eighteen tunnels
had to be built through the Sierra
Mountains before the railroad could
cross from California into Nevada.

NEVADA

"The Silver State" became the 36th State, 1864

 NEVADA was the last of our western states to be explored. The land seemed nothing but desert wilderness, discouraging to the homesteader. Only sagebrush grew in the valleys, and for the cattle there was only bunch grass to feed on. A small band of Mormons settled there in 1849.

Then in 1859, settlers began pouring into the lonely Nevada Territory. What drew them? The discovery of the Great Comstock Lode! Suddenly the mining town of Virginia City boomed, and for thirty years the amazing Comstock Lode produced over a billion dollars' worth of gold and silver.

Nevada is today one of our largest states, but one of the most thinly populated. More than half the people live in the two largest cities, Reno and Las Vegas. Fewer people live in Carson City than in almost any other state capital.

Nevada might well say of itself, "How dry I am." Less rain falls here than in any other state. The moisture-laden winds from the Pacific Ocean cannot cross its western wall of mountains—the snow-capped Sierra Nevadas. On the land, too dry to be farmed, great herds of cattle, horses and sheep graze.

The landscape is strange and beautiful. Nevada shares with California the eerie desert of Death Valley and deep, deep Lake Tahoe, set high in the hills. To the north are dying volcanoes, hot springs and geysers. One hot spring runs into a cool mountain stream. Fishermen claim they can catch a fish in the cool stream and cook it in the hot spring without taking it off the hook!

NEW HAMPSHIRE

"The Granite State" became the 9th State, 1788

IN 1776 New Hampshire became the first colony to set itself up as an independent state. Folks in nearby Maine and Massachusetts shook their heads in admiration, and said New Hampshirites were as tough as the granite in their White Mountains.

They *were* tough and they had good sense. They looked around and saw that their rock-ribbed, hilly state would be hard to farm. But they also saw the water power that could be harnessed from their great rivers foaming down the mountains. So the people of New Hampshire built mills and factories along the river shores. They used the rivers to turn wheels and move machinery. New Hampshire factories have been busy ever since making cloth, paper, shoes and machine parts. And today manufacturing is the most important industry in the state.

Not everyone in New Hampshire works in factories. New Hampshire does have farms—farms that raise hay and dairy herds, chickens and eggs. And farms that grow berries, apples and peaches. The farmers sell most of their chickens and dairy products to New Hampshire hotels to feed hungry vacationers.

Vacationers are a big business in New Hampshire. If you've ever had a New Hampshire vacation, you know why so many people go there for summer fun and winter sports. Who wouldn't enjoy hiking over green woodland trails, camping in the deep woods, or skiing down the snowy slopes of the White Mountains?

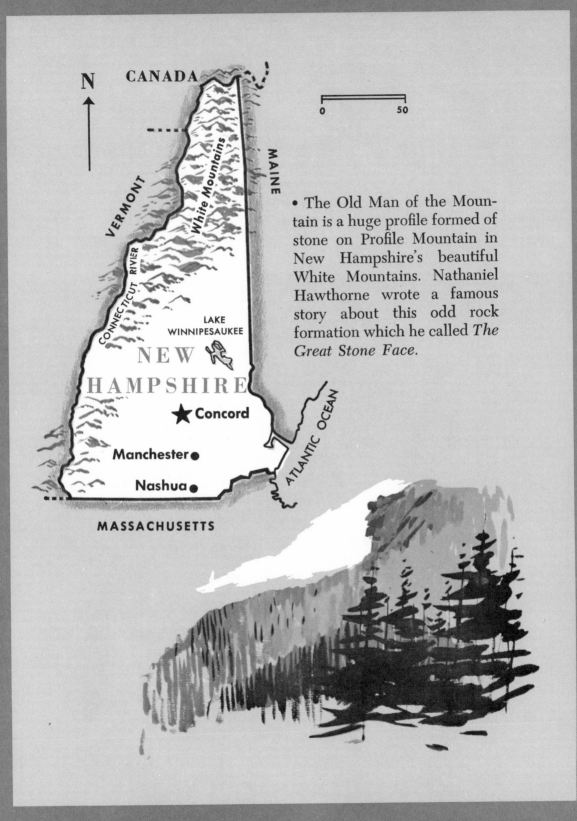

N

CANADA

VERMONT

White Mountains

Connecticut River

MAINE

LAKE WINNIPESAUKEE

NEW HAMPSHIRE

★ Concord

Manchester ●

Nashua ●

ATLANTIC OCEAN

MASSACHUSETTS

0   50

• The Old Man of the Mountain is a huge profile formed of stone on Profile Mountain in New Hampshire's beautiful White Mountains. Nathaniel Hawthorne wrote a famous story about this odd rock formation which he called *The Great Stone Face*.

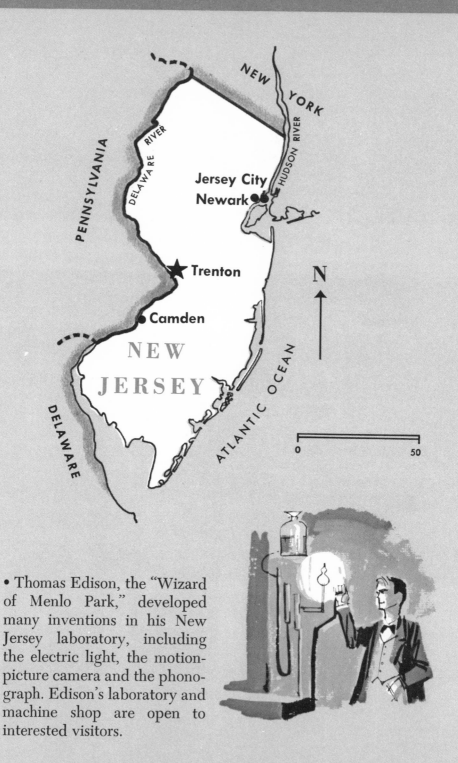

NEW JERSEY

PENNSYLVANIA

DELAWARE RIVER

NEW YORK

HUDSON RIVER

Jersey City
Newark

★ Trenton

● Camden

DELAWARE

ATLANTIC OCEAN

N

0   50

• Thomas Edison, the "Wizard of Menlo Park," developed many inventions in his New Jersey laboratory, including the electric light, the motion-picture camera and the phonograph. Edison's laboratory and machine shop are open to interested visitors.

NEW JERSEY

"The Garden State" became the 3rd State, 1787

 FARMS and factories, superhighways and dirt roads, mountains and beaches, port cities and fishing villages—you can find them all in New Jersey, one of our smallest states.

New Jersey is almost an island, and its waterways have always been important. In pioneer days, its rivers were highways and gateways to inland America. Today ocean liners, freighters and tankers from all over the world sail into the deep, broad harbors of Newark, Camden, Trenton, Jersey City and Hoboken.

New Jersey has at least 50 million neighbors—including the people of New York City and Philadelphia. These good neighbors are good customers, too. They buy the products from New Jersey's factories and farms.

These products are astonishingly varied. The oil in your furnace, the paint and varnish on your furniture, your radio, too, may have come from New Jersey. No other state produces so many chemical products. Manufacturing is by far New Jersey's most important business, but the "Garden State" raises all kinds of crops, too. It is said that New Jersey farms produce everything from apples to zucchini!

Many a battle took place on New Jersey soil during the Revolutionary War. One of the most famous was the Battle of Trenton. This was fought on Christmas night in 1776. Leading his troops across the icy Delaware River, General Washington gave the enemy Hessian soldiers an unexpected Christmas surprise!

NEW MEXICO

"Land of Enchantment" became the 47th State, 1912

SQUARE-SHAPED New Mexico is a combination of the old and the new, of Indian, Spanish and American ways of life. Navaho and Pueblo Indians were here long before the Spaniard Coronado came in 1540. Today one hears both English and Spanish in New Mexico.

In New Mexico one is always reminded of the past. In Gallup, Indians still dance their ancient tribal dances. In Santa Fe, oldest capital city in the U.S., there are buildings 350 years old. Reminders of the future are just as strong. In the desert at White Sands, scientists experiment with rockets. At the Lovelace Clinic in Albuquerque they test the astronauts, our first space men.

You don't often need a raincoat in sunny New Mexico. This is a dry land and water is very precious. The waters of the Rio Grande flow through the entire state, but many irrigation projects are also needed for the farms that grow corn, wheat and cotton.

Sheep and cattle raising are important here. So is mining for copper, lead, silver and gold. New Mexico leads the nation in the production of uranium and potash.

Almost everywhere in New Mexico you can see mountain peaks. Children who go to the public schools in Santa Fe get skiing lessons in the Sangre de Cristo Mountains.

In this "Land of Enchantment" one of the most magical places is Carlsbad Caverns. This is the largest group of connected underground caves ever discovered. Scientists say they were formed 60 million years ago.

64

COLORADO

OKLAHOMA

Rocky Mountains

★ Santa Fe

● Gallup

● Albuquerque

ARIZONA

NEW MEXICO

N

RIO GRANDE RIVER

● Roswell

WHITE
SANDS
DESERT

CARLSBAD
CAVERNS ▲

TEXAS

MEXICO

0   100

• Long before Columbus found the New World, Indians built pueblo villages in New Mexico. Made of sun-dried brick, these pueblos rose like "apartment houses" on flat-topped hills. To get from one level to another, ladders were used. Some pueblos had as many as a thousand rooms. Zuni and Hopi Indians today live in pueblos as their ancestors did.

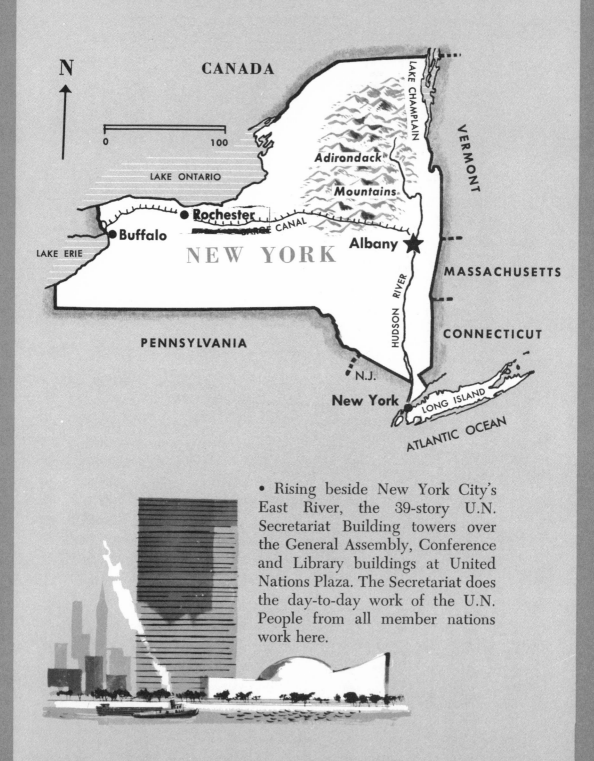

N

CANADA

0   100

LAKE ONTARIO

LAKE CHAMPLAIN

VERMONT

Adirondack

Mountains

Rochester

BARGE CANAL

Albany

MASSACHUSETTS

Buffalo

LAKE ERIE

NEW YORK

HUDSON RIVER

CONNECTICUT

PENNSYLVANIA

N.J.

New York

LONG ISLAND

ATLANTIC OCEAN

• Rising beside New York City's East River, the 39-story U.N. Secretariat Building towers over the General Assembly, Conference and Library buildings at United Nations Plaza. The Secretariat does the day-to-day work of the U.N. People from all member nations work here.

NEW YORK

"The Empire State" became the 11th State, 1788

 IN 1626 the Dutch bought Manhattan Island from the Indians. Guess what they paid? Twenty-four dollars. Guess what that land is worth today? About thirty billion dollars! For Manhattan is now the center of New York City—the largest city in the Americas.

New York's harbor handles more freight than any other port in the Western Hemisphere, and there are always at least 150 ships at its piers. New York City has the most hotels, museums, broadcasting stations, clothing factories, banks and publishing houses of any city in America. Here, too, are the Empire State Building—one of the world's tallest buildings—the Statue of Liberty and the United Nations.

More than a third of the battles of the Revolutionary War were fought in New York State. After the war, many settlers moved to the fertile inland valleys of central and western New York. Later they shipped their produce to eastern cities down the Erie Canal on barges towed by horses. Expanded and deepened, the Erie is now part of New York's great Barge Canal. Tugs do the work that horses used to do.

New York State has more than a dozen major industrial cities. But vineyards and orchards flourish in its valleys, and its dairy farms rank high in milk production. New York City attracts the most visitors, but vacationers also throng to the state's lovely lakes and mountains.

For 150 years the Empire State had the largest population of any state, but in 1963 California took first place. Over eighteen million people now live in New York State.

NORTH CAROLINA

"The Tarheel State" became the 12th State, 1789

THE first English colony in North America was a lost colony. Even before the Jamestown settlement, even before the Pilgrims landed on Plymouth Rock, English ships had sailed to the coast of what is now North Carolina. They brought a colony of 150 people who settled on Roanoke Island. When the ships returned three years later, everyone in the colony had vanished—including Virginia Dare, the first child born of English parents in America.

Many a ship was lost, too, off the dangerous North Carolina coast. Sailors had good reason to fear stormy Cape Hatteras, which they called the "Graveyard of the Atlantic."

The coast of North Carolina may be stormy, but inland the landscape is peaceful and lovely. In the east are fertile plains and rising in the west are the Appalachian Mountains. With neighboring Tennessee, North Carolina shares one of the most popular vacation sites in the nation—Great Smoky Mountains National Park. The smoky blue haze over the mountains gives the Smokies their name.

Only Texas has more farms than North Carolina. And on this rich land, farmers raise cotton, corn, tobacco, soybeans, fruit, and peanuts. North Carolina scientists have developed an atomic peanut. They call it NC 4X. These extra-large peanuts are grown from seeds exposed to atomic radiation.

No other state produces as much tobacco, textiles and softwood lumber. So it's not surprising that North Carolina also has the largest hosiery mills and cigarette factories in the world, and makes much of the nation's furniture.

68

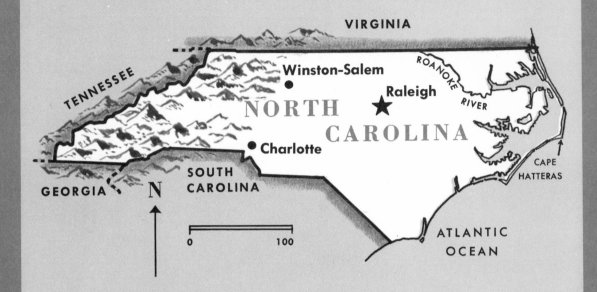

• The first flight in a power-driven airplane was made by Wilbur and Orville Wright at Kitty Hawk Beach on December 17, 1903. This flight lasted only 12 seconds. Five years later Wilbur set a new world's record by flying a plane 52 miles and staying aloft for over an hour. A monument stands at Kill Devil Hill near Kitty Hawk Beach to mark the scene of the first plane flight.

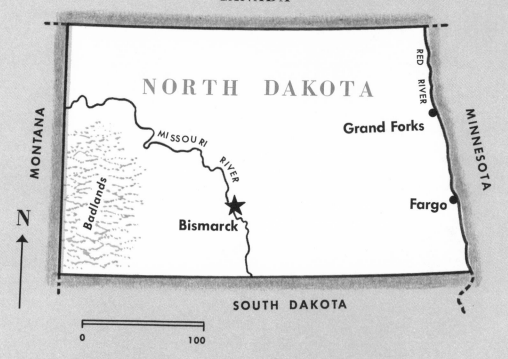

CANADA

NORTH DAKOTA

MONTANA

Badlands

MISSOURI RIVER

RED RIVER

Grand Forks

MINNESOTA

Fargo

★ Bismarck

N

SOUTH DAKOTA

0   100

• Sacagawea was a young Indian squaw. In 1804, she joined the expedition of Lewis and Clark not far from where Bismarck stands today. She guided them, helped them deal with the Indians and led them safely across the mountains. This statue of Sacagawea stands on the capitol grounds at Bismarck.

NORTH DAKOTA

"The Flickertail State" became the 39th or 40th State, 1889

THE Great Dakota Mystery will never be solved. Until 1889, North and South Dakota made up the Dakota Territory. Then both joined the Union as separate states. Which one was admitted first? No one will ever know. For President Harrison deliberately shuffled the two state proclamations before signing them.

Before 1850, farming was difficult in much of North Dakota. Then it was discovered that wheat would flourish in the Red River Valley. Soon railroads were built to bring in the thousands of settlers who came to farm the vast prairies. Ever since, the Red River Valley has been one of the great wheat-growing regions of the world.

The ranches of North Dakota are big, too. Although there is snow in the winter, cattle and sheep can range all year. The sweet clover blossoms that grow on the plains have made possible a profitable bee-keeping industry.

The broad Missouri River can be seen from the 18-story capitol building in Bismarck. There is still a log cabin on these modern capitol grounds—the cabin where Theodore Roosevelt lived during 1883.

The Dakota Indians believed there were demons lurking among the weird stone peaks in the Badlands of North Dakota. The underground "furnace" near Amidon must have seemed especially like demon's work. Veins of lignite coal burn here, giving off a reddish glow which can be seen for miles. These veins light themselves, after being wet by the rain and then dried out by the sun.

OHIO

"The Buckeye State" became the 17th State, 1803

FOR almost two hundred years, Ohio was the crossroads of a growing America. Pioneers came by canoe across Lake Erie, by barge and keelboat up the Ohio River. They came from the South and they came from New England. The New Englanders called their new Ohio towns by the names they had left behind—Norwalk and New London. The southerners built white-pillared homes in towns they called Gambier and Mount Vernon. And beside Lake Erie, Moses Cleveland built a town.

Cleveland is now Ohio's largest city and the state's chief steel-making center. Although Ohio has no iron of its own, steel is a major industry. The iron ore brought by way of Lake Erie feeds the great steel mills of Cleveland, Steubenville, Youngstown, and Lorain.

Ohio and industry go hand in hand. Columbus, the capital city, produces aircraft and machinery. Cincinnati, busy port on the Ohio River, has a large printing industry. Dayton makes the nation's cash registers, and Toledo its scales. From Akron come most of the tires for America's cars.

Ohio is rich in natural resources—coal, limestone, oil and timber. Toledo is one of the most important coal-shipping ports in the world. And from the clay deposits come the pottery and porcelain for which Ohio's southeastern cities are famous. The soil, too, is rich and yields a harvest of corn and grapes and tobacco.

Ohio has sent eight of its sons to the White House—Grant, Hayes, Garfield, McKinley, Taft, Harding and two Harrisons.

72

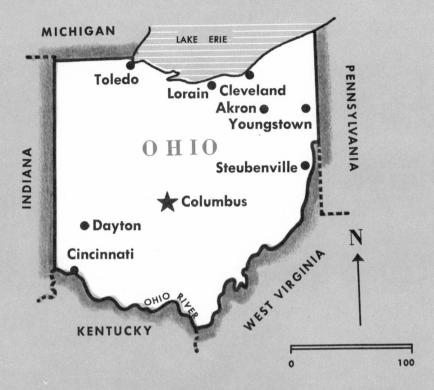

MICHIGAN

LAKE ERIE

PENNSYLVANIA

Toledo

Lorain Cleveland
Akron
Youngstown

OHIO

Steubenville

INDIANA

★ Columbus

● Dayton

Cincinnati

N

WEST VIRGINIA

OHIO RIVER

KENTUCKY

0   100

• Ohio has been a fruit-growing state since pioneer
days when "Johnny Appleseed" wandered through
the territory, planting his apple trees. His real name
was John Chapman.

COLORADO KANSAS MISSOURI

NEW MEXICO

N

0   100

Oklahoma City
★

Tulsa

ARKANSAS RIVER

OKLAHOMA

ARKANSAS

RED RIVER

TEXAS

• You could almost spell Oklahoma O-I-L! There's so much oil that oil well derricks even dot the Capitol grounds in Oklahoma City. One big oil strike took place in 1920 on land held by the Osage Indians.

OKLAHOMA

"The Sooner State" became the 46th State, 1907

IT is April 22, 1889. In wagons and prairie schooners, eager homesteaders wait for a pistol shot. Crack! The Oklahoma Territory is open! The rush for land is on. Within twenty-four hours 50,000 settlers have staked their claims. Some homesteaders jumped the gun, however, and entered the territory sooner. That is how Oklahoma earned its nickname—the Sooner State.

It was the Indians, though, who named Oklahoma—their word for *Land of the Red People.* When parts of the territory were opened to white settlers, the Indians were moved to land in Oklahoma that no one wanted. It was a lucky move. In 1920 oil was discovered on this very land.

Oil is now Oklahoma's most important business. More than 700 petroleum companies have their headquarters in Tulsa, often called "The Oil Capital of the World." And in Oklahoma City, the capital, people have even discovered oil in their backyards!

Oklahoma is rich in other minerals, too—natural gas, coal and zinc. And its fertile farms yield wheat, rye, cotton and the largest crop of broomcorn in the U.S. On the ranches of Oklahoma, cowboys herd cattle, sheep, horses—even turkeys! Cowboys are so important in Oklahoma that a monument dedicated to them stands in front of the Capitol building in Oklahoma City.

Oklahoma is shaped somewhat like a saucepan. Doesn't the narrow strip to the west look like the handle of the pan? That's what it's called—the *Panhandle.*

OREGON

"The Beaver State" became the 33rd State, 1859

NOT long ago a skeleton was dug up in central Oregon. It was the skeleton of a mighty brontosaurus—fifty feet from head to tail! Perhaps it lived on the giant palms and ferns that flourished when Oregon was a prehistoric jungle.

In those ancient times the highest mountains were volcanoes, and a terrific volcanic explosion blew the top off one great mountain peak. The hole which is left, almost half a mile deep, is filled today with the blue waters of Crater Lake. Oregon's highest peak, Mt. Hood, is an inactive volcano.

From the dense forests that cover the lower slopes of Oregon's mountains comes much of America's lumber. Under parts of these forests lie treasures of gold and silver.

Oregon's Snake River has the deepest canyon in the country. Irrigation projects in the Snake River Valley have turned a former desert into fertile grain- and vegetable-growing country. Western Oregon is one of the world's great fruit-growing regions.

The great Columbia River, which the Indians called *Ouragan,* serves Oregon well. The huge Bonneville Dam on the Columbia generates electric power for homes and factories. The Dam has also helped make the Columbia an important river highway, for ocean-going ships can now sail inland 100 miles, past Portland. The Columbia River is also a "highway" for the salmon that keep Oregon's fisheries and canneries busy. Fish ladders—a step-like series of pools—help the salmon go upstream past the Columbia's dams.

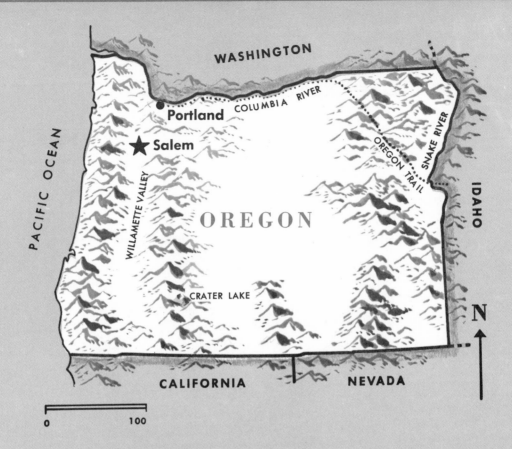

• In the 1840's and '50's, thousands of pioneers took the Oregon Trail, bound for free land in Oregon's Willamette Valley. The trail was America's longest overland route, 2,000 hard, dangerous miles. Parts of it, rutted by wagon wheels, can still be seen.

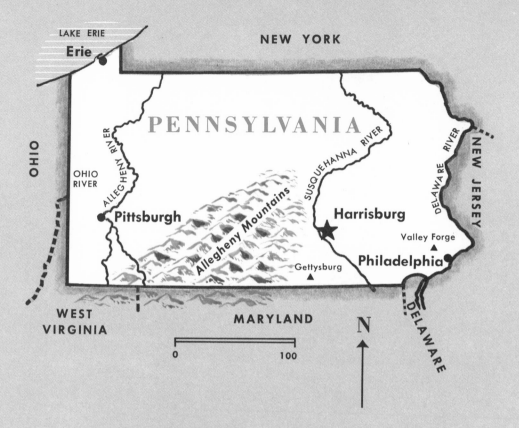

LAKE ERIE
Erie

NEW YORK

OHIO

OHIO RIVER

ALLEGHENY RIVER

PENNSYLVANIA

SUSQUEHANNA RIVER

DELAWARE RIVER

NEW JERSEY

Pittsburgh

Allegheny Mountains

Harrisburg

Valley Forge ▲

Gettysburg ▲

Philadelphia

WEST VIRGINIA

MARYLAND

DELAWARE

0   100

N

• The Liberty Bell in Philadelphia's Independence Hall rang to announce the adoption of the Declaration of Independence in 1776. The bell is inscribed: "Proclaim Liberty throughout all the land, unto all the inhabitants thereof."

PENNSYLVANIA

"The Keystone State" became the 2nd State, 1787

 The riddle: Why is Philadelphia's City Hall called the biggest penholder in the world?
The answer: Because the top of the City Hall holds a statue of William Penn that's 37 feet tall!

William Penn is tall indeed in the history of this state. A Quaker himself, he founded a colony where all could worship as they pleased. The first settlement, Philadelphia—now fourth largest city in our nation—is still called the City of Brotherly Love.

Meet another citizen of Pennsylvania—Mike Fink the keelboatman, born in Pittsburgh in 1770. Many a pioneer heading west or south was carried down the Ohio River on Mike's keelboat. Today the Ohio carries freight barges laden with iron and steel from Pittsburgh's great mills.

Pennsylvania is one of the top-ranking industrial states in the Union. About one-fourth of the nation's steel is produced here, and only West Virginia and Kentucky mine more coal. Pennsylvania's hills are rich in other minerals, too—in oil and natural gas, iron and limestone.

And American history has roots deep in Pennsylvania soil. In Valley Forge, George Washington held together a cold and hungry army in the cruelest winter of the Revolutionary War. The Declaration of Independence was adopted in Philadelphia's Independence Hall. And it was in dedicating the bloody battleground of Gettysburg that Abraham Lincoln told the world that "government of the people, by the people, for the people, shall not perish from the earth."

RHODE ISLAND

"Little Rhody" became the 13th State, 1790

HOW small is our smallest state? Only 48 miles long and 37 miles wide! You could fit 220 Rhode Islands into Texas! But if you compared one average square mile in each of our states, you'd find that Rhode Island, in relation to its size, is the second most densely populated state in the Union.

Rhode Island has a proud history, and was founded on a great freedom—the freedom of worship. In 1636 Roger Williams established the settlement of Providence and offered shelter to all who wished to worship in their own way. In the struggle for independence, Rhode Islanders played a bold role. In 1772, when the British ship *Gaspee* came to collect taxes, they set the ship afire. So impatient was Rhode Island to be free, they announced their independence of British rule three months before the Declaration of Independence was accepted by the Continental Congress. Later they passed the first law in America forbidding the bringing in of slaves from Africa. There is a statue atop the Capitol building in Providence called Independent Man. He seems the very spirit of Rhode Island!

Because the state was small and its farmland poor, most Rhode Islanders turned to manufacturing to make a living. Manufacturing history was made in America when the first spinning jenny went into operation in 1790. Today the making of textiles is Rhode Island's leading industry. Its factories also produce machinery and rubber goods, and it is a major producer of silverware and jewelry.

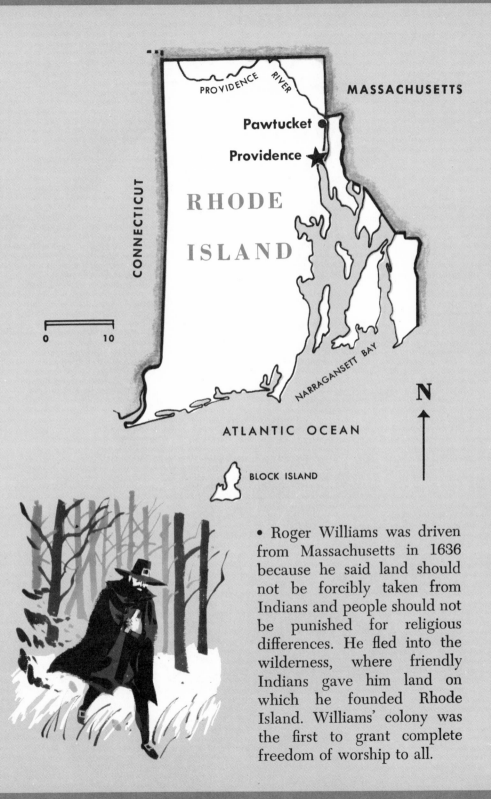

RHODE ISLAND

PROVIDENCE RIVER

MASSACHUSETTS

Pawtucket

Providence

CONNECTICUT

0   10

NARRAGANSETT BAY

ATLANTIC OCEAN

N

BLOCK ISLAND

• Roger Williams was driven from Massachusetts in 1636 because he said land should not be forcibly taken from Indians and people should not be punished for religious differences. He fled into the wilderness, where friendly Indians gave him land on which he founded Rhode Island. Williams' colony was the first to grant complete freedom of worship to all.

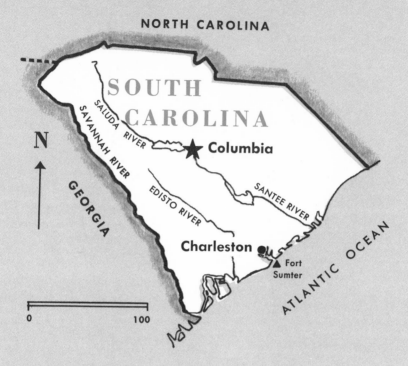

NORTH CAROLINA

SOUTH
CAROLINA

SALUDA RIVER
SAVANNAH RIVER

N

★ Columbia

GEORGIA

EDISTO RIVER

SANTEE RIVER

Charleston ●

▲ Fort
Sumter

ATLANTIC OCEAN

0   100

• South Carolina became the first state to secede
from the Union when Lincoln was elected in 1860.
The first shot of the Civil War was fired on Fort
Sumter in Charleston Harbor on April 12, 1861.

SOUTH CAROLINA

"The Palmetto State" became the 8th State, 1788

 PIRATE ground! Back in the 1700's South Carolina's inlets and marshes and islands were used as hideouts for bloodthirsty buccaneers like Blackbeard.

In those days English settlers brought roots and seeds to plant in the fertile soil of the new colony. On the plantations that sprawled beyond the lovely town of Charleston, colonists raised rice and the indigo used to make blue dyes for cloth that was also woven in South. Carolina.

Today Charleston is a beautiful port city with many formal gardens and mansions, some over 200 years old. Ships sail out of her busy harbors crammed with bales of cotton, for cotton has long been South Carolina's leading crop. Much of this cotton stays behind in South Carolina, however, to be made into cloth. Huge cotton crops and cheap water power from swift-running rivers have helped to make South Carolina one of the nation's leading textile manufacturers. Its busy mills produce wool, rayon, nylon and orlon, as well as cotton fabrics.

Rich soil makes it possible for South Carolina farmers to harvest tobacco, peaches, oats, sweet potatoes, peanuts and corn. They raise hogs, cows and chickens, too. And at Sumter you'll find the largest pigeon farm in the world.

The British colony of Carolina was named for Charles I. So was Charleston. But the "Palmetto State" won its nickname *fighting* a British king—George III. In a fort built of palmetto logs on an island in South Carolina, a small band of patriots won the first victory of the Revolutionary War.

SOUTH DAKOTA

"Sunshine State" became the 39th or 40th State, 1889*

SOUTH DAKOTA'S bones are world famous! For strange creatures once lived there—tiny three-toed horses and saber-toothed tigers. Their fossilized bones have been found in the White River Badlands, and shown in museums around the world. The Badlands are famous, too—over a million acres of weird landscape.

The Missouri River flows through South Dakota for more than 500 miles, almost cutting the state in two. To the west of the river are the plains and the great grassy ranches where herds of cattle and sheep graze. East of the Missouri, where the soil is fertile and the rainfall good, flat fields of corn and wheat seem to stretch to the sky's edge. Potatoes and hardy fruit like apples grow well here, too.

In the southwest are the beautiful Black Hills. They might well have been called "Gold Hills." Custer's men discovered gold here in 1847, and since then these mountains have yielded precious metal worth millions of dollars. Homestake Mine, at Lead, is one of the largest gold mines in the world.

Today most visitors come to the Black Hills to see the largest sculptures ever made by man. These are the huge stone faces of Washington, Jefferson, Lincoln and Theodore Roosevelt. Carved out of the granite sides of Mount Rushmore, each head is in proportion to men 465 feet tall.

South Dakota's capital, Pierre, was once a small trading post, and the first governor of South Dakota was William Jayne. Governor Jayne was also a doctor. Who was his most famous patient? Abraham Lincoln!

* See North Dakota, p. 71.

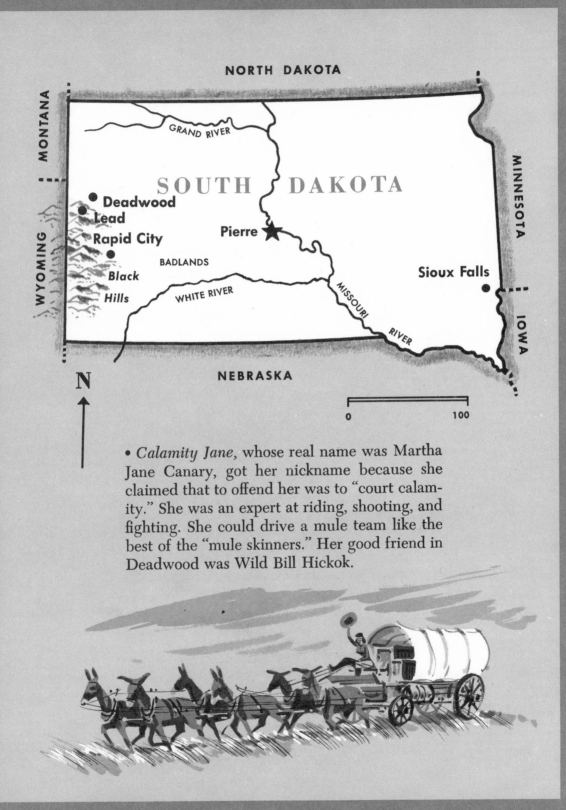

NORTH DAKOTA

MONTANA

GRAND RIVER

SOUTH DAKOTA

MINNESOTA

WYOMING

• Deadwood
• Lead
Rapid City
BADLANDS
Black
Hills
WHITE RIVER

Pierre ★

Sioux Falls
•

MISSOURI RIVER

IOWA

NEBRASKA

N

0   100

• *Calamity Jane,* whose real name was Martha Jane Canary, got her nickname because she claimed that to offend her was to "court calamity." She was an expert at riding, shooting, and fighting. She could drive a mule team like the best of the "mule skinners." Her good friend in Deadwood was Wild Bill Hickok.

• Davy Crockett was born in the Great Smoky Mountains in East Tennessee, in 1786. He served his country as a soldier and Indian scout. Tennessee voters elected him to Congress three times. His motto, "Be sure you're right, then go ahead," became known all over the nation.

TENNESSEE

"The Volunteer State" became the 16th State, 1796

THE three stars in Tennessee's flag stand for three parts of the state. If you ask a native of Tennessee where he lives he may say East or Middle or West Tennessee. In the *East* rise the Great Smoky Mountains. Here mountaineers farm their crops on hills so steep that harvests often have to be hauled away on sleds. Coal deposits are found in East Tennessee, too. *Middle Tennessee,* lying in the Cumberland foothills, is rolling and hilly. Here cattle, sheep and horses graze on grassy land. And *West Tennessee,* between the Mississippi and the winding, bending Tennessee River, is a land of white cotton fields.

The rich valleys of Tennessee always drew the farmers, even in pioneer days. But in time the soil became less fertile. Too much cotton raising wore out the land. Floods washed away the rich topsoil. In 1933, Congress set up TVA— the Tenneesee Valley Authority. TVA built dams to control the floods and restore the land. TVA also created water power for new industries. Today factories along the riverbanks process food, make chemicals and manufacture textiles. Tennessee also produces marble and important minerals, including coal and zinc.

Tennessee has four cities where more than 100,000 people live—Memphis, Nashville, Chattanooga and Knoxville. The newest city in the state is Oak Ridge. Here, in the greatest secrecy, part of the first atomic bomb was made. The project was so secret people didn't even know there *was* an Oak Ridge until the end of World War II.

TEXAS

"The Lone Star State" became the 28th State, 1845

TEXAS was once an independent nation. It became a republic after General Sam Houston defeated the Mexican forces in 1836. Shortly after, Texas elected Sam Houston president of the "Republic of Texas" and named its largest city, Houston, in his honor.

You need the word LARGEST to describe Texas. Texas is our second largest state. The largest state fair is held in Dallas every October. The largest rose-growing center in the world is near Tyler. The largest state capitol building is at Austin, capital of Texas. And the irrigation program in Texas is vast, too—with many large projects along the coast and in the lower Rio Grande below Falcon Dam.

You need the word MOST, too. For Texas has the most farms in the U.S. and raises the most cattle and sheep on its great ranches. Texas grows the most rice, cotton and spinach, and produces a fourth of the nation's oil.

Remember the Alamo? The famous old mission building known as the "Alamo" still stands in San Antonio. Here Davy Crockett, Jim Bowie and other brave men fought to the death for the freedom of Texas.

There were pirates as well as heroes in Texas's past. It was the buccaneer Jean Lafitte who founded the port city of Galveston on the Gulf of Mexico. Galveston Island was his headquarters until the U.S. Navy drove him out.

There's only one star in the flag of the Lone Star State. But it stands for stirring moments in American history.

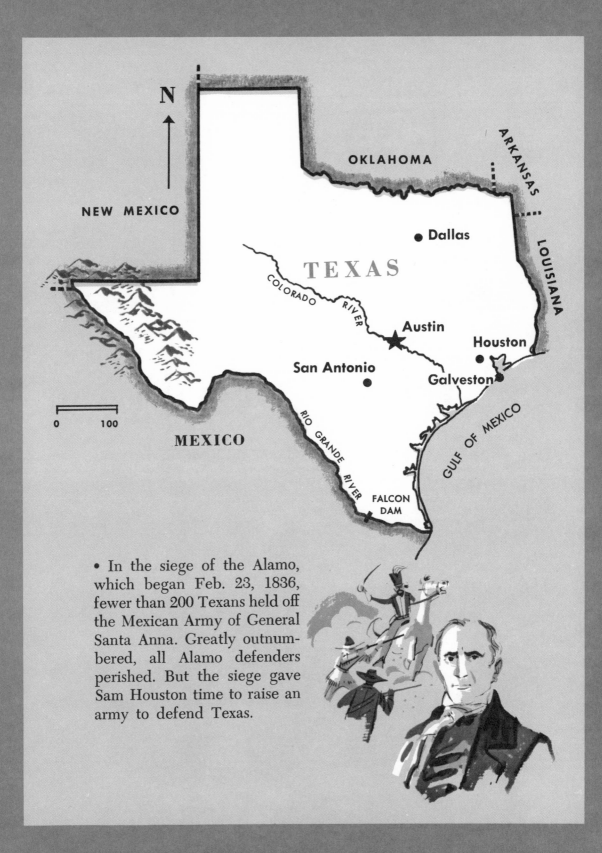

N

OKLAHOMA

NEW MEXICO

ARKANSAS

LOUISIANA

• Dallas

TEXAS

COLORADO RIVER

Austin

Houston

San Antonio

Galveston

0   100

MEXICO

RIO GRANDE RIVER

GULF OF MEXICO

FALCON
DAM

• In the siege of the Alamo, which began Feb. 23, 1836, fewer than 200 Texans held off the Mexican Army of General Santa Anna. Greatly outnumbered, all Alamo defenders perished. But the siege gave Sam Houston time to raise an army to defend Texas.

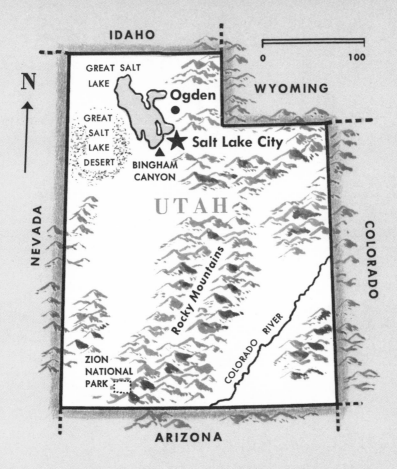

IDAHO

WYOMING

N

GREAT SALT
LAKE

● Ogden

0   100

GREAT
SALT
LAKE
DESERT

★ Salt Lake City

BINGHAM
CANYON

NEVADA

UTAH

COLORADO

Rocky Mountains

COLORADO RIVER

ZION
NATIONAL
PARK

ARIZONA

• James Bridger, fur trapper and scout, was the first white man to see Utah's Great Salt Lake. When he came upon the lake's vast stretches of shining water in 1824, Bridger thought at first that he had reached the shores of the Pacific.

UTAH

"The Beehive State" became the 45th State, 1896

THE Great Salt Lake Valley stretching ahead seemed nothing but desert and mountains. But to the band of weary Mormons seeking freedom of worship, it was the promised land. "This is the place," said Brigham Young, their leader. That very day—July 24, 1847—the Mormons unhitched their oxen and planted potatoes.

The Mormons made the Utah desert blossom with their irrigation methods. They dug ditches and channels and turned the streams so water would flow where it was needed. Today thousands of acres of fertile soil produce grains, fruits and vegetables. But manufacturing is Utah's most important industry, with food and metal products leading the parade. Gold, silver, lead, zinc, uranium, coal—its hills are filled with treasure. Especially copper! There's a mountain of copper ore at Bingham Canyon.

Utah is an inland state, far from the Atlantic and Pacific Oceans. Then where does that good sea smell of salt spray come from? From the clear green waters of Great Salt Lake near Salt Lake City—waters saltier than the ocean. Swimming there is fun, for you can't sink. The salt keeps you afloat.

Utah has many other natural wonders, carved and shaped by wind and water. Rainbow Bridge in southeastern Utah is the largest natural bridge in the world. And strangely colored canyons, deserts and gorges fill the National Parks—Zion Park and Bryce Canyon—with weird beauty.

Utah's weather is a natural wonder, too—clear and dry 300 days out of the year.

VERMONT

"Green Mountain State" became the 14th State, 1791

 VERMONT is well named. It was the French, led by Champlain, who first explored here, and in their language *vert mont* means *green mountain.*
Fast-running streams and rivers tumble down these green mountains—rivers that mean water power for Vermont's factories. From these factories come machine tools, weighing scales and woolen goods. From Vermont's forests and saw-mills and woodworking plants come lumber and pulp for the making of paper. And in the hills are layers of asbestos, slate and fine building stone. United Nations headquarters in New York City was built of Vermont marble, and the state's own handsome capitol at Montpelier is made of native granite.

Despite its rocky soil, Vermont does much farming. Vermont's maple syrup is famous everywhere. Indians made the first syrup. They notched the maple trees and caught the sweet sap in birch-bark buckets. Today many Vermont farmers have sugar maple trees. The Indians would be astonished by the plastic pipes and tin containers used today, but they would recognize the old delicious flavor. You can see Vermont "sugaring" from early March to mid-April.

Vermont is a favorite vacation place. People come to see the peaceful farms and historic towns. They camp in the mountains in the summer and ski down its trails in the winter.

Some visitors return to stay. Rudyard Kipling liked Vermont so much he built a home in Brattleboro, where he wrote for many years. Have you ever read *The Jungle Book*? The story took place in India but Kipling wrote it in Vermont!

CANADA

LAKE
CHAMPLAIN

● **Burlington**

Montpelier
★

VERMONT

NEW YORK

▲ Fort Ticonderoga

● **Rutland**

NEW HAMPSHIRE

Green Mountains

N

0 ___ 50

● **Brattleboro**

MASSACHUSETTS

• At dawn on May 10, 1775, Ethan Allen and his Green Mountain Boys—a force of Vermont volunteers—captured Fort Ticonderoga, N.Y., from the surprised and sleepy British. Allen demanded they surrender "in the name of Jehovah and the Continental Congress."

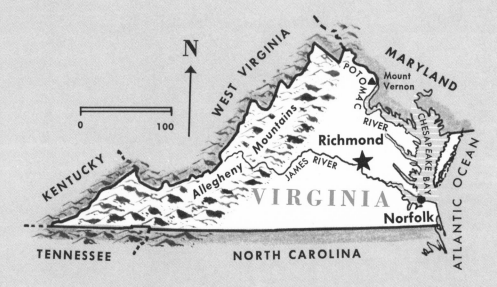

• George Washington's happiest years were spent on his estate at Mount Vernon, overlooking the Potomac River. There, as a gentleman farmer, he grew large crops of grain and tobacco. Visitors to Mount Vernon today can wander through the rooms of Washington's stately home, furnished as they were when he lived there.

VIRGINIA

"The Old Dominion" became the 10th State, 1788

ONE of the biggest birthday parties in the U.S. is held every year in Virginia. What does it celebrate? The landing of Captain John Smith and his band of hardy colonists at Jamestown in 1607, and the settlement of the first permanent English colony in America.

Luckily, these colonists had a good neighbor in Pocahontas, the Indian princess. It is said that she saved Captain Smith's life and taught the English how to grow tobacco. It has been the main crop ever since. The Indians taught the English how to plant corn and peanuts, too.

The eastern part of Virginia—the Tidewater region—was once covered by ocean. And the ocean tide still pushes back up Virginia's broad rivers. These rivers empty into Chesapeake Bay, forming excellent harbors. Norfolk is on the most important harbor in the state; this harbor, called Hampton Roads, could hold all the great navies of the world.

The ships that sail these rivers carry cargoes of textiles, coal, corn, hams, apples, dairy products and cigarettes—all from the mines, farms and factories of Virginia.

The beauty of Virginia's hills and valleys has been sung in many a song. It would take a spooky tune, though, to tell of the Great Dismal Swamp with its weird trees and bogs, black bears and wildcats.

Traveling in Virginia is like stepping back into history. Four of our first five presidents came from Virginia. And the countryside is dotted with memorials to great men and great battles.

WASHINGTON

"The Evergreen State" became the 42nd State, 1889

WHAT contains enough concrete to pave a four-lane highway from Seattle to New York? What do engineers call "the biggest job on earth"? The answer is "Grand Coulee," largest of the dams which turn the Columbia River's fast-flowing waters into electric power for Washington's homes, farms and industries.

The state is famous for its salmon fishing and canning, but of even more value now is the manufacturing of machinery, ships, wood and food products, and aircraft. The Hanford atomic energy plant near Richland is of great importance to the country in the space age.

The Columbia River is over a thousand miles long. The great Cascade Mountains of Washington also seem endless. These mountains run down Washington like a wall—dividing the state in two and creating two climates. West of the Cascades the weather is mild and rainy. Here are the vast forests that feed Washington's great lumber mills. East of the Cascades, the weather is very different. For the mountain wall cuts off the Pacific breezes. There is less rainfall and many farms in the central part of the state must be irrigated.

Seattle was a small town when Washington became a state. It had a fine harbor on Puget Sound. Then gold was found in the Yukon in 1896 and Seattle began to grow. It became a busy outfitting station for prospectors bound for the gold fields. Today Seattle is Washington's largest city. Olympia, the capital, is also located on Puget Sound. The Sound is a gateway for trade with ports in Asia and Alaska.

CANADA

RIVER

GRAND
COULEE DAM

Spokane

Seattle

PUGET
SOUND

Mountains

COLUMBIA

WASHINGTON

IDAHO

PACIFIC OCEAN

Tacoma

Olympia

Cascade

N

OREGON

0   100

• Washington is famous for its sockeye salmon fishing and for its other fishing industries. Seattle, one of the largest salmon markets in the world, handles fish from both Washington and Alaska.

N

Wheeling ●

PENNSYLVANIA

OHIO

OHIO RIVER

MARY-
LAND

POTOMAC RIVER

WEST
VIRGINIA

Allegheny Mountains

★ Charleston

● Huntington

VIRGINIA

KENTUCKY

0   50

• Coal deposits lie under some two-thirds of West Virginia's rocky surface. Many West Virginia workers earn their living by mining coal. Coal was first discovered in the state by John P. Salley in 1742 and was in use about 1810 to heat homes and make steel in Wheeling.

WEST VIRGINIA

"The Mountain State" became the 35th State, 1863

 UNTIL 1861, West Virginia was a region in Virginia, separated from the rest of the state by the Allegheny Mountains. When the Civil War began, Virginia became part of the Confederacy. West Virginia seceded from Virginia and joined the Union as a separate state.

If a reporter had interviewed the first West Virginia settlers, he might have reported this conversation:

"How do you plan to make a living here?"

"We'll start farms. Most of us are farmers."

"But there's not much level ground. Look around you—hills and mountains everywhere."

"Then we'll plant our crops on the slopes or graze our cattle, hogs and sheep. Those of us who don't farm might go into the salt business. We've watched the Indians make salt from salt-water pools. We've seen them collect all the salt left after the pools dried up."

Today West Virginia's salt deposits are necessary to one of its largest industries—the manufacture of chemicals. West Virginia still farms—especially fruit. One of the largest apple-growing areas in America is the Shenandoah Valley.

In West Virginia they tell tall tales about John Henry, the steel-driving man—John Henry, who drove the steel for the Big Bend railroad tunnel up in the Allegheny Mountains.

And there are many tunnels in the mountains of West Virginia. Most of them lead into the sunless corridors of coal mines, for West Virginia produces the most soft, or bituminous, coal in the nation.

WISCONSIN

"The Badger State" became the 30th State, 1848

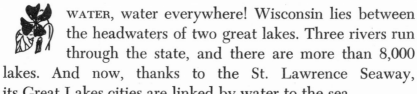 WATER, water everywhere! Wisconsin lies between the headwaters of two great lakes. Three rivers run through the state, and there are more than 8,000 lakes. And now, thanks to the St. Lawrence Seaway, its Great Lakes cities are linked by water to the sea.

Wisconsin is famous as the "Dairyland of the Nation," for it produces most of our milk and cheese. Have you ever heard of cheese-wrestling? No, it isn't a sport, and you won't see it on TV. It's part of the work of cheese-making in the city of Monroe. There workers really "wrestle" big 250-pound wheels of cheese as they rub them with salt.

Wisconsin does have plenty of sports—skiing and ice-boating, fishing and hunting. The state has many kinds of game birds and animals. However, its nickname comes not from badger-hunting, but from lead-mining. Years ago, miners in Wisconsin were called "badgers." They lived in caves that reminded people of badgers' burrows.

Wisconsin's state government has been a leader in the making of laws to improve working and living conditions. It was the first state to pass laws providing for pensions for mothers and teachers, payments to workers injured on their jobs, payments to unemployed people and pensions for old people. Wisconsin has also been a leader in setting up co-operatives where people can buy and sell goods at a saving.

Fox Indians called the part of Wisconsin they lived in "Delightful Land." This area is now Milwaukee, Wisconsin's largest city and a leading Great Lakes port.

100

LAKE SUPERIOR

0   100

MICHIGAN

MINNESOTA

ST. CROIX RIVER

MISSISSIPPI RIVER

WISCONSIN

GREEN BAY

La Crosse

WISCONSIN RIVER

LAKE MICHIGAN

N

IOWA

Madison ★ Milwaukee

Monroe

Racine

ILLINOIS

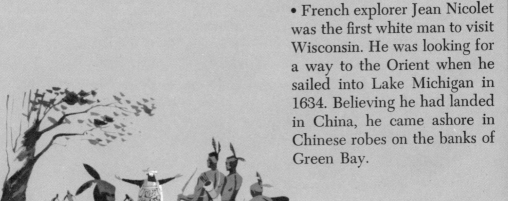

• French explorer Jean Nicolet was the first white man to visit Wisconsin. He was looking for a way to the Orient when he sailed into Lake Michigan in 1634. Believing he had landed in China, he came ashore in Chinese robes on the banks of Green Bay.

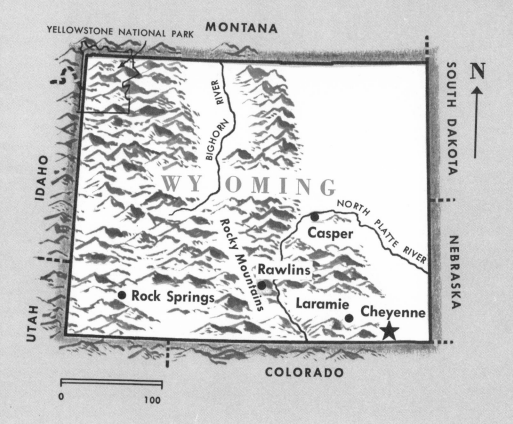

YELLOWSTONE NATIONAL PARK MONTANA

IDAHO

SOUTH DAKOTA

N

BIGHORN RIVER

WYOMING

NORTH PLATTE RIVER

● Casper

Rocky Mountains

● Rawlins

NEBRASKA

● Rock Springs

● Laramie ● Cheyenne ★

UTAH

COLORADO

0   100

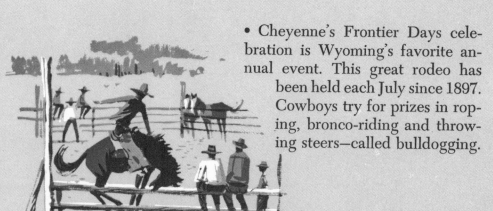

• Cheyenne's Frontier Days cele-
bration is Wyoming's favorite an-
nual event. This great rodeo has
been held each July since 1897.
Cowboys try for prizes in roping, bronco-riding and throw-
ing steers—called bulldogging.

WYOMING

"The Equality State" became the 44th State, 1890

 JETS of hot water shoot hundreds of feet into the air. Streams of cold water and streams of boiling water run side by side down high mountains. Where is this land of fire and ice? In Yellowstone National Park in Wyoming, a region of spouting geysers, mountains, rivers and lakes.

Less than a hundred years ago, Wyoming was still frontier land. In 1867, the railroad reached what is now Cheyenne. Then towns sprang up—Laramie, Rawlins, Rock Springs. Cheyenne, growing rapidly, became the state capital.

There is much in Wyoming to remind you of its frontier past. Cowboys still drive herds of cattle over wide, grassy plains. Hundreds of sheep graze on great open ranges. Rodeos and roundups are held every July in Cheyenne.

Long ago, the Cheyenne Indians soaked twigs in puddles of oil on the ground. Presto! They had torches. They did not know that someday oil wells would rise above these puddles, bringing up enough oil to fill millions of barrels a year.

Wyoming is rich in other natural resources, too. About five million tons of soft coal are mined each year and more iron ore is produced in Wyoming than in any other Rocky Mountain state. The first major uranium discovery in Wyoming occurred in 1951. By the late 1950's, Wyoming ranked third among the states in known uranium reserves.

It's easy to understand why tourists are Wyoming's second largest industry. They come for the sport and the scenery— for the big game hunting and the dude ranches, and for the awe-inspiring beauty of the national parks.

ALASKA

Today people go to the beautiful "land of the midnight sun" for vacations. Many choose Alaska as a place to make their homes. No one thinks of it as "a dreary waste of glaciers and icebergs."

But when our Secretary of State, William H. Seward, arranged to buy Alaska from Russia back in 1867, most Americans said it was a bad bargain. They called it "Seward's Folly," "Seward's Icebox," and other names.

Before long, Americans knew that Mr. Seward was right to buy that land. It cost $7,200,000. By 1903, Alaska had paid back $9,555,909 in taxes and other revenues to the United States government. And Alaska's fish, furs, and gold were worth almost $150,000,000.

The southern part of Alaska is a long strip along the Pacific coast, called the Panhandle. It is a maze of hundreds of islands. They rise in mountain peaks along the Pacific Coast near Juneau, the state capital. If you took a trip there, you might be reminded of pictures of the steep, craggy coast of Norway.

Islands make up a good part of this big new state. Those called the Aleutian Islands stretch like stepping stones from Asia to America. Some scientists think that Mongolian tribes from Asia came by way of Bering Strait and the Aleutians to settle in America. They believe that these were the people

Totem pole carved by Tlingit Indians.

living all over America when Columbus arrived, thousands of years later. He called them Indians.

Today there are three groups of Indians in Alaska —all with different languages and customs. The Athabascans live on the mainland. The Haidas live on islands off the coast of the Panhandle. And the Tlingits live in the Panhandle itself. These seafaring Indians adorn their cedar houses with totem poles. They are also fine carvers of stone and workers of copper.

The best-known natives of Alaska are the Eskimos. Their relatives, the Aleuts, live in the Aleutian Islands.

Eskimos hunting a whale off Alaska's coast.

Planning to visit the Aleutians? If you go to the island of Unalaska, be sure to take your rain gear. This island is one of the rainiest places in the United States. It has rain or snow, on the average, five days out of every week.

Perhaps you have enjoyed the antics of polar bears in a zoo. At home on Alaska's shores and waters, they do amazing stunts. They travel on ice too thin to hold up a man who weighs 500 or 600 pounds *less* than a polar bear. How do the bears do it? By spreading their legs well apart to distribute the weight—and by keeping on the move. When the ice is very thin, the bear lies on its belly and pulls itself along by its claws.

Polar bears have an acute sense of smell. Men of our Navy tell of visits by these great white bears when a ship rides at anchor. Sitting on some sea ice or padding along the beach, a bear may smell cooking and swim to the ship for a handout.

Probably the noisiest sea animal in the state—or in the entire United States—is the walrus. Even when it is a baby, its bark is as loud as that of a grown St. Bernard dog. The walrus also trumpets like an elephant. When a herd of a hundred walruses gather on shore and start to bellow and trumpet, they can make more noise than a hundred tooting horns in a traffic jam.

Noisy or not, the Eskimo needs the walrus as much as the Indians of our western plains needed the buffalo. To the Eskimo, the walrus is important for food, clothing and shelter, just as the buffalo was to the plains Indians.

"Only seals welcome." This might well be the sign around the Pribilof Islands. When Alaska fur seals were almost wiped out by the many hunters, the government turned these islands into a reservation for seals. People are not allowed on the islands without special permission. And ships are not allowed to land there except in emergency.

Do you dream of life on the range? Perhaps you'd like to be a reindeer herder. In the past, many Alaskan natives

Fur seals in the government reservation on the Pribilof Islands.

depended on the caribou for food, winter clothing, and summer tents. When the caribou were almost gone, the government imported reindeer from Siberia. Herding reindeer is a year-round, open-range job.

American defenses in Alaska are united by an early-warning and communications system. It also links Alaska

Mount McKinley, highest peak of North America

The great antennas of White Alice permit dependable telephone communication throughout Alaska.

closely with the rest of the United States. This is the Distant Early Warning radar network, known as the Dew Line. In 1958 the radar net was improved by a new system for radio transmission, called White Alice. For Alaskans living in remote areas, White Alice now permits dependable telephone communication.

The Alaskans have been called "the flyingest people under the American flag." Lacking other means of getting about that big land, they took to the air. Planes can carry people and all the things they need. Pilots have learned to land on beaches, sand bars, rivers, lakes or—with planes equipped with skis—on icy strips and snow-covered tundras.

The larger cities of Alaska are linked by one or more airlines with daily jet service. Most towns and many villages have daily service by regularly scheduled airline.

A scientific laboratory on a floating island! That's Fletcher's Ice Island. It drifts about in the Arctic Ocean near Point Barrow, the point farthest north in the United States. Here, on a 4-mile chunk of floating ice, is a station of the University of Alaska's Arctic Research Laboratory.

HAWAII

A Hawaiian fisherman casts a great net, as his Polynesian ancestors did.

The natives of Hawaii are called Polynesians. They received the name from the first white men to explore the islands of the Pacific. On Hawaii and many islands to the south, the explorers found people who were similar in looks, language, and culture. So the white men made up a Greek name for them—*polys*, meaning many, plus *nesos*, meaning island. Or, as we would say in English, "many island" people.

Nearly every kind of plant can grow in our newest state. People and animals can thrive here, too. One thing lacking is minerals. Because they had no iron or metal, the Polynesians used bamboos for blades and polished stones for adzes. They used shells to cut and scoop. Digging with sticks, they planted taro, yams, sweet potatoes and bananas.

Hawaiians have a traditional feast which visitors enjoy. It's called a *luau*. The food is cooked in a pit on hot stones. There are always roast pork, fish and chicken. There are many dishes wrapped in banana leaves, as well as coconuts, pineapples and other fruits. At a truly native *luau*, there is *poi*, a paste made by mixing taro root with water. It is eaten with the fingers.

Robert Louis Stevenson, the author of *Treasure Island*, liked to sail among the islands of the Pacific. He stayed for six months in Hawaii. There he visited a heroic Belgian missionary priest, Father Damien, who had volunteered to live among the lepers. A colony for lepers had been set up on the northern coast of the island of Molokai. At that time, medical science had no cure for leprosy. But modern drugs are now proving effective against the disease.

Perhaps you have seen little Oriental boxes made of sweet-smelling sandalwood. Originally this wood came from Hawaii. Today there is scarcely a stick of it left in all the islands. During the days of whaling, one clever ship's captain noticed the sweet-smelling wood and took some with him on his voyage to China.

The Chinese liked it so much for incense and cabinet work that they wanted to buy more of it. A trade sprang up in sandalwood. Before long almost all the wood had been cut down. It became so scarce that full-rigged ships were given to island chiefs in exchange for the precious wood.

Queen Liliuokalani reigned from 1891 to 1893.

Queen Liliuokalani ascended the throne early in 1891. She wrote the best known of all Hawaiian songs, "Aloha Oe." She held a magnificent court and kept all the ancient ceremonies. But times were changing. In 1893, Hawaii became a republic. Then its government asked to be taken in as a territory of the United States.

Some of the largest privately developed irrigation projects are in Hawaii. Entire plateaus have been changed from wasteland into some of the most valuable farming land in the world. Tens of thousands of acres, little used in the past, now produce sugar.

The reason for the development of irrigation systems is that sugar needs a great deal of water to grow. To produce one pound of sugar takes 2,000 pounds of water. One irrigation ditch in one of the great irrigation projects, for instance, carries up to 60,000,000 gallons of water daily. Another even larger project supplies more than 300,000,000 gallons a day—more than four times the amount of water used daily by a city almost as big as San Francisco.

In spite of all the land used to grow pineapple and sugar cane, Hawaiian cattle ranches cover more space than all the plantations together. Some of the world's largest ranches are

Terraced pineapple fields. Three-fourths of the world's pineapple comes from Hawaii.

located here. There are typical western cowboys on the islands of Maui and Hawaii. It all started in 1783 when Captain George Vancouver brought in a few cattle. The Hawaiian chiefs gave the cattle royal protection. The cattle ran wild and increased in great numbers.

Then, about a hundred years ago, three Mexican cowboys were brought in to herd the cattle. They started a way of life that captured the imagination of the Hawaiians. Boys and young men donned chaps and sombreros, mounted horses, and learned to toss ropes. Soon more than half the cowboys were Hawaiian, and the rest Japanese and Portuguese.

Hawaiian roundup—on the world's second largest Hereford cattle ranch.

The native dance of Hawaii is the hula. It is a beautiful dance in which the hands tell the story in a sort of pantomime. Many of the stories are traditional, while others are made up by the dancer with special hand motions for each dance. The hands may speak, for example, of birds in flight. Or they may turn slowly to show leaves moving in the wind.

Mauna Loa's fountain of lava, erupting hundreds of
feet above the nearby trees.

On Hawaii, the Big Island, the volcano Mauna Loa has
erupted many times. One evening in November of 1959, it
erupted again. Lava came boiling and bubbling out of a
mile-long crack. On hand were the scientists of Hawaiian Volcano Observatory, as well as many people from Hilo, Honolulu and other places. A volcanic eruption in Hawaii is a
spectacle for all to go to see.

The scientists, armed with instruments, went down into
the crater to collect samples of volcanic gases and red-hot
lava. They learned a great deal about the inside of the earth,
what volcanoes are, what makes them erupt.

Mauna Loa continued to erupt for a month. Once a fountain of lava rose higher than the Empire State Building in
New York. The scientists kept going back throughout the
month to gather information. They considered it the best
opportunity they had ever had to learn more about volcanoes.

115

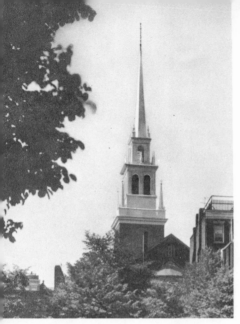

Old North Church is one of many
historic landmarks in Boston.

Toolmaker at work. New England was the
birthplace of American manufacturing.

NEW ENGLAND

A covered bridge built in Maine over 100 years ago.

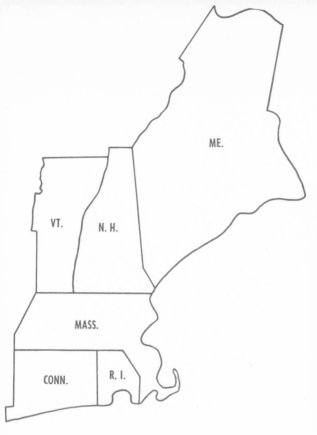

Sugaring in Vermont. Sap from the maple is made into syrup and candy.

Fisherman mends net. Fleets of trawlers fish with these big nets.

Historic moment at Groton, Conn.—launching of the first atomic submarine, the *Nautilus*, in 1954.

The port of New York—busiest harbor in the world.

MIDDLE ATLANTIC

Customs of Pennsylvania Amish people have not changed much over the years.

A ship going through one of the locks of the 182-mile St. Lawrence Seaway.

Clothes begin with patterns. New York
leads in manufacture of clothes.

Pittsburgh is one of the nation's
chief steel-making cities.

STATES

New Jersey raises many vegetables
for the markets of nearby cities.

N. Y.

PA.

N. J.

MD.

W. VA.

DEL.

Many boys and girls in the Middle
West raise prize livestock.

The skyline of Chicago,
first city of the Middle West.

MIDDLE WEST

Farm machinery, like these combines, is needed on the huge wheat fields of Kansas.

Famous Wisconsin cheese
is stored to ripen.

On a Detroit assembly line today—
on the nation's roads tomorrow.

A stern-wheeler begins its journey down the Mississippi.

A mechanical cotton picker works
fast in an Alabama cotton field.

SOUTHERN
STATES

In Louisiana, cypress trees and
oil wells rise side by side.

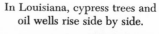

Kentucky's famous thoroughbred horses.

Texas cattle moving to the summer range.

Spraying a grove of citrus trees.

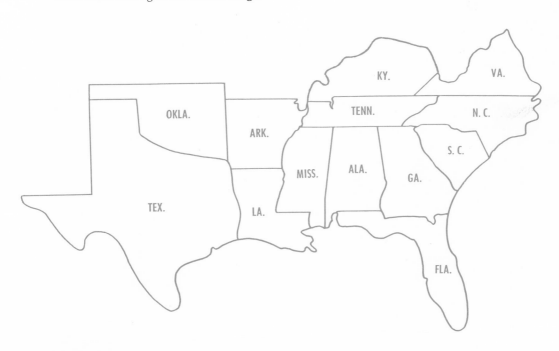

A cowboy ropes a calf at a Wyoming rodeo.

MOUNTAIN STATES

This falcon is the mascot of the
U.S. Air Force Academy in Colo.

The saguaro cactus may grow 50 feet tall.

Hoover Dam is shared by
Arizona and Nevada.

A modern prospector uses his Geiger
counter to track uranium in New Mexico.

A giant tree will soon begin its
journey to an Oregon sawmill.

PACIFIC
COAST

A dramatic panorama of Death Valley.

Pineapples, one of Hawaii's big crops,
are harvested by modern machinery.

This Eskimo's kayak is made of wood
and sealskin. Scene: Alaska.

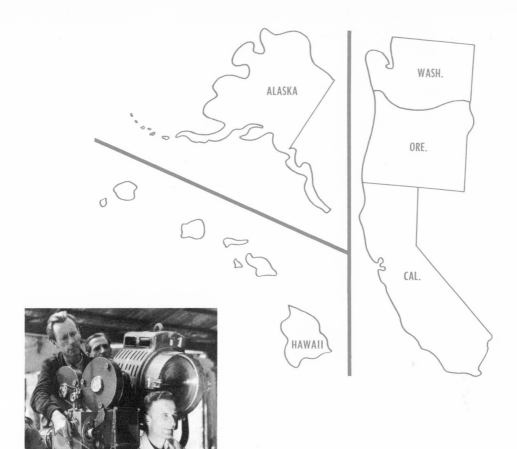

ALASKA

WASH.

ORE.

CAL.

HAWAII

Movie-making in Hollywood.

Fresh crab cooked while you wait at
Fisherman's Wharf in San Francisco.

Fishing for salmon with hoop
nets on the Columbia River.

FIFTY STATES UNDER ONE FLAG

The American flag was adopted by the Continental Congress on June 14, 1777. It had thirteen stripes and thirteen stars—one for each of the original states. Since then, a new star has been added for each new state. Now, together with the original thirteen stripes, the American flag has fifty stars.

Nine months after its adoption, the new flag received its first salute from a foreign nation. This flag had been made by young ladies in Portsmouth Harbor, New Hampshire, from their own and their mothers' dresses. John Paul Jones, the great naval hero, raised the flag on his ship *Ranger*. When the *Ranger* sailed into a harbor on the coast of France, the French admiral gave the new flag a salute of nine guns.

During the War of 1812, the British fleet tried to capture Fort McHenry, which guarded the city of Baltimore. When they bombarded the fort in 1814, Francis Scott Key was with the British fleet. He had gone there to get a friend who was held prisoner. All night Key watched the battle. When he saw the American flag still flying the next morning, he wrote "The Star-Spangled Banner." This song became our national anthem by an act of Congress, approved by President Herbert Hoover on March 3, 1931.

HOW AMERICA GREW

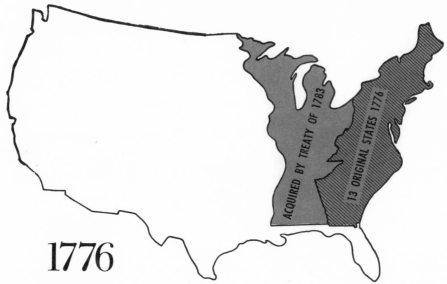

1776

13 original states: Mass., N.H., R.I., Conn., N.Y., N.J., Pa., Del., Md., Va., N.C., S.C., Ga. *Treaty of 1783 became:* Ohio, Ind., Ill., Mich., Wis., Ky., Tenn., parts of Miss., Ala., Minn.

1803

Louisiana Purchase became: Iowa, Mo., Ark., Nebr., parts of La., Okla., Kans., N. Dak., S. Dak., Mont., Wyo., Colo., Minn. *1818:* Territory ceded by Great Britain became: parts of N. Dak., S. Dak., Minn. *1819:* Florida Purchase (from Spain) became: Fla., parts of Ala., Miss., La.

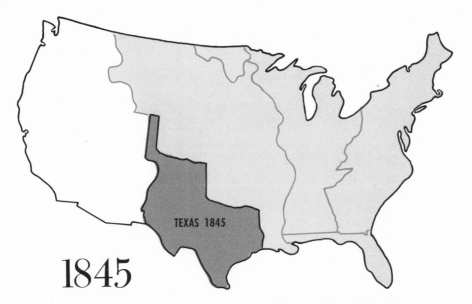

1845

Texas Annexation became: Tex., parts of Kans., Okla., N. Mex., Colo., Wyo.

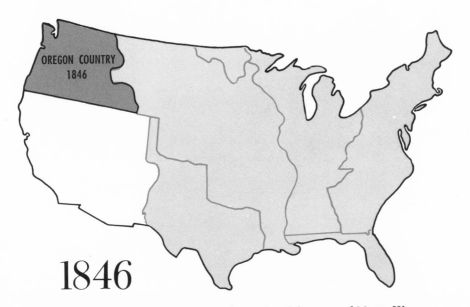

1846

Oregon Country Annexation became: Oreg., Wash., Idaho, parts of Mont., Wyo.

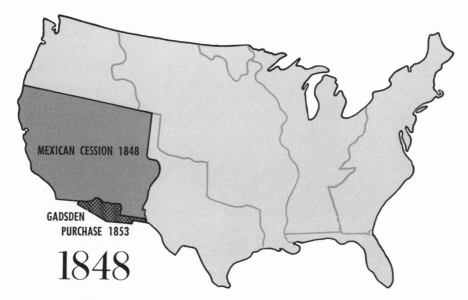

1848

Mexican Cession became: Calif., Nev., Utah, parts of Ariz., Colo., Wyo., N. Mex.
Gadsden Purchase from Mexico became: parts of N. Mex., Ariz.

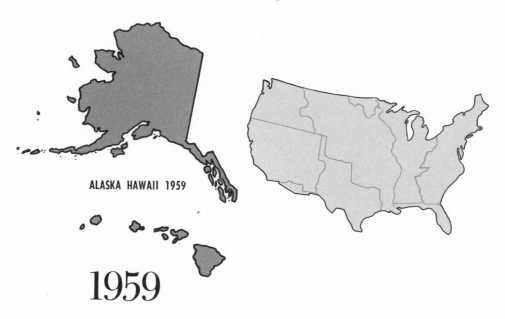

1959

In 1959 the U.S. admitted Alaska and Hawaii to statehood.

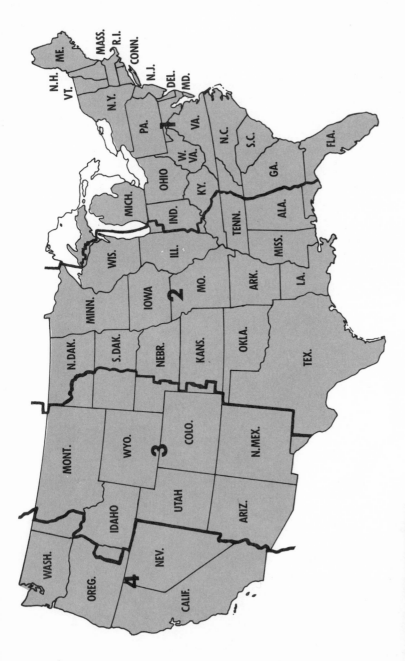

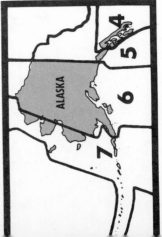

SET YOUR CLOCK

Continental U.S.A. has four time zones—1. Eastern Standard Time, 2. Central Standard Time, 3. Mountain Standard Time and 4. Pacific Standard Time. Alaska has three additional time zones—5. Yukon Time Zone, 6. Alaska Time Zone and 7. Bering Time Zone. Hawaii is in the Alaska Time Zone. Each time zone is one hour earlier when you move from east to west.

At 12:00 noon in New York City it's 9:00 A.M. in Seattle, Washington.

STATE BIRDS AND FLOWERS

ALABAMA	Yellowhammer	Camellia
ALASKA	Willow Ptarmigan	Forget-me-not
ARIZONA	Cactus Wren	Saguaro Cactus
ARKANSAS	Mockingbird	Apple Blossom
CALIFORNIA	Valley Quail	Golden Poppy
COLORADO	Lark Bunting	Columbine
CONNECTICUT	Robin	Mountain Laurel
DELAWARE	Blue Hen Chicken	Peach Blossom
FLORIDA	Mockingbird	Orange Blossom
GEORGIA	Brown Thrasher	Cherokee Rose
HAWAII	Hawaiian Goose	Hibiscus
IDAHO	Mountain Bluebird	Lewis Mock Orange
ILLINOIS	Cardinal	Violet
INDIANA	Cardinal	Peony
IOWA	Eastern Goldfinch	Wild Rose
KANSAS	Western Meadowlark	Sunflower
KENTUCKY	Cardinal	Goldenrod
LOUISIANA	Brown Pelican	Magnolia
MAINE	Chickadee	Pine Cone
MARYLAND	Baltimore Oriole	Black-eyed Susan
MASSACHUSETTS	Chickadee	Mayflower
MICHIGAN	Robin	Apple Blossom
MINNESOTA	Loon	Showy Lady's-slipper
MISSISSIPPI	Mockingbird	Magnolia
MISSOURI	Bluebird	Hawthorn
MONTANA	Western Meadowlark	Bitterroot
NEBRASKA	Western Meadowlark	Goldenrod
NEVADA	Mountain Bluebird	Sagebrush
NEW HAMPSHIRE	Purple Finch	Purple Lilac
NEW JERSEY	Eastern Goldfinch	Violet
NEW MEXICO	Road Runner	Yucca
NEW YORK	Bluebird	Rose
NORTH CAROLINA	Cardinal	Flowering Dogwood
NORTH DAKOTA	Western Meadowlark	Wild Prairie Rose
OHIO	Cardinal	Scarlet Carnation
OKLAHOMA	Scissor-tailed Flycatcher	Mistletoe
OREGON	Western Meadowlark	Oregon Grape
PENNSYLVANIA	Ruffed Grouse	Mountain Laurel
RHODE ISLAND	Rhode Island Red	Violet
SOUTH CAROLINA	Carolina Wren	Yellow Jessamine
SOUTH DAKOTA	Ring-necked Pheasant	Pasqueflower
TENNESSEE	Mockingbird	Iris
TEXAS	Mockingbird	Bluebonnet
UTAH	Gull	Sego Lily
VERMONT	Hermit Thrush	Red Clover
VIRGINIA	Cardinal	Flowering Dogwood
WASHINGTON	Willow Goldfinch	Coast Rhododendron
WEST VIRGINIA	Cardinal	Rhododendron
WISCONSIN	Robin	Violet
WYOMING	Meadowlark	Indian Paintbrush

The official flower of the District of Columbia is the American Beauty Rose;
its bird, the Woodthrush.

STATE AREAS AND POPULATIONS

STATE	POPULATION	RANK IN POPULATION	REPRESENTATIVES	ELECTORAL VOTES	AREA (SQUARE MILES)	RANK IN AREA
Alabama	3,444,165	21	7	9	51,609	29
Alaska	302,173	50	1	3	586,412	1
Arizona	1,772,482	33	4	6	113,909	6
Arkansas	1,923,295	32	4	6	53,104	27
California	19,953,134	1	43	45	158,693	3
Colorado	2,207,259	30	5	7	104,247	8
Connecticut	3,032,217	24	6	8	5,009	48
Delaware	548,104	46	1	3	2,057	49
District of Columbia	756,668				68	
Florida	6,789,443	9	15	17	58,560	22
Georgia	4,589,575	15	10	12	58,876	21
Hawaii	769,913	40	2	4	6,450	47
Idaho	713,008	42	2	4	83,557	13
Illinois	11,113,976	5	24	26	56,400	24
Indiana	5,193,669	11	11	13	36,291	38
Iowa	2,825,041	25	6	8	56,290	25
Kansas	2,249,071	28	5	7	82,264	14
Kentucky	3,219,311	23	7	9	40,395	37
Louisiana	3,643,180	20	8	10	48,523	31
Maine	993,663	38	2	4	33,215	39
Maryland	3,922,399	18	8	10	10,577	42
Massachusetts	5,689,170	10	12	14	8,257	45
Michigan	8,875,083	7	19	21	58,216	23
Minnesota	3,805,069	19	8	10	84,068	12
Mississippi	2,216,912	29	5	7	47,716	32
Missouri	4,677,399	13	10	12	69,686	19

STATE AREAS AND POPULATIONS

STATE	POPULATION	RANK IN POPULATION	REPRESENTATIVES	ELECTORAL VOTES	AREA (SQUARE MILES)	RANK IN AREA
Montana	694,409	43	2	4	147,138	4
Nebraska	1,483,791	35	3	5	77,227	15
Nevada	488,738	47	1	3	110,540	7
New Hampshire	737,681	41	2	4	9,304	44
New Jersey	7,168,164	8	15	17	7,836	46
New Mexico	1,016,000	37	2	4	121,666	5
New York	18,241,266	2	39	41	49,576	30
North Carolina	5,082,059	12	11	13	52,586	28
North Dakota	617,761	45	1	3	70,665	17
Ohio	10,652,017	6	23	25	41,222	35
Oklahoma	2,559,253	27	6	8	69,919	18
Oregon	2,091,385	31	4	6	96,981	10
Pennsylvania	11,793,909	3	25	27	45,333	33
Rhode Island	949,723	39	2	4	1,214	50
South Carolina	2,590,516	26	6	8	31,055	40
South Dakota	666,257	44	2	4	77,047	16
Tennessee	3,924,164	17	8	10	42,244	34
Texas	11,196,730	4	24	26	267,338	2
Utah	1,059,273	36	2	4	84,916	11
Vermont	444,732	48	1	3	9,609	43
Virginia	4,648,494	14	10	12	40,817	36
Washington	3,409,169	22	7	9	68,192	20
West Virginia	1,744,237	34	4	6	24,181	41
Wisconsin	4,417,933	16	9	11	56,154	26
Wyoming	332,416	49	1	3	97,914	9

U.S. Census figures (1970)

DID YOU KNOW
THAT IN THE U.S. . . . ?

. . . the oldest and largest tree is called "General Sherman" and

grows in California . . . the longest river is the Missis-

sippi (2,348 miles) . . . the largest city is New York City . . . the

coldest spot is Tanana, Alaska . . . the largest active

volcano is Mauna Loa in Hawaii . . . the largest natural bridge is

Rainbow Bridge in Utah . . . our largest lake is Lake

Superior . . . the wettest spot is Mt. Waileale in Hawaii (record:

642 inches of rain in one year) . . . our smallest state

is Rhode Island . . . the largest man-made hole is the open-pit

MEN
WORKING

mine at Mesabi, Minnesota . . . the widest glacier

is Malaspina Glacier in Alaska . . . the lowest point is Death Valley,

California . . . the least rain falls in Nevada

. . . our largest and oldest national park is Yellowstone National

Park . . . the most peanuts are raised in Georgia . . .

our largest desert is the Mojave in California . . . our largest state

is Alaska . . . the largest popcorn-processing plant is in Iowa

. . . the only state pronounced as one syllable is Maine

and Ask, Me., is a town there . . . some towns are named for

chemicals—Carbon, Calcium, Cobalt and Soda . . . the largest

silver mine is in Idaho . . . our oldest town is St. Augustine,

Florida . . . the highest mountain is Mt. McKinley in Alaska

(20,320 feet) . . . the highest waterfall is

Yosemite Falls in California

INDEX

Abilene, Kans., *34*, 35
Adams, John, 19
Adirondack Mountains, *66*
Akron, Ohio, 72, *73*
Alabama, *2, 3*
Alamo, 88, 89
Alaska, *4, 5*, 96, 104–9, *131*
Albany, N.Y., 67
Albuquerque, N. Mex., 65
Aleutian Islands, 104, 105, 106
Allegheny Mountains, *78, 94, 98*, 99
Allegheny River, *78*
Allen, Ethan, 93
Amish people, *118*
Anchorage, Alaska, 5
Aniakchak Volcano, 4
Annapolis, Md., *42*, 43
Appalachian Mountains, 68
Arbor Day, 57
Arco, Idaho, *26*, 27
Arctic Ocean, 5
Arctic Research Laboratory, 109
Arizona, *6, 7*
Arkansas, 8, 9
Arkansas River, 8, 9, 12, *13, 34*, 74
Astronauts, tested at Lovelace Clinic, 64
Athabascans, 105
Atlanta, Ga., 22
Augusta, Me., *41*

Badlands, Dakota, 71, 84
Baltimore, Md., *42*, 43
Baton Rouge, La., *38*, 39
Bauxite, 8
Bear, Kodiak, 5, *5*
Bering Sea, 5
Bering Strait, *5*, 104
Big Black River, *50*
Biloxi, Miss., *50*
Bingham Canyon, Utah, 90, 91
Birmingham, Ala., *2, 3*
Bismarck, N. Dak., 70, *70*
Black Hills, S. Dak., 84
Block Island, *81*
Boise, Idaho, *26*, 27
Bonneville Dam, 76
Boone, Daniel, 36, 37
Boonesborough, Ky., 36, *37*
Boston, Mass., 44, *45*
Bowie, Jim, 88
Brattleboro, Vt., 92, *93*

Bridgeport, Conn., *14*, 15
Bridger, James, 90
Bryce Canyon, Utah, 91
Buffalo, N.Y., *66*
Bunker Hill, Battle of, 44
Bunyan, Paul, 49, *49*
Bureau of Engraving and Printing, 19
Burlington, Vt., *93*
Butte, Mont., *54*, 55

Cactus, 7, *124*
Calcasieu River, *38*
California, *10*, 11
Camden, N.J., *62*
Canary, Martha Jane, 85
Canaveral, Cape, 21, *21*
Cape Cod, *45*
Cape Hatteras, 68
Cape Elizabeth Lighthouse, 41, *41*
Capitol, 18, *18*
Car manufacture, in Mich., 46, 47, *121*
Carlsbad Caverns, 64, *65*
Carson City, Nev., 57, 58
Cascade Mountains, 96, 97
Casper, Wyo., *102*
Cattle-raising in Texas, 88, *123*
Cedar Rapids, Iowa, 33
Central Pacific Railroad, 58
Chalk Bluff, Ark., 8
Champlain, Lake, *66, 93*
Chapman, John, 73
Charleston, S.C., 82, *82*, 83
Charleston, W.Va., 98
Charlotte, N.C., 69
Charter Oak, *14*
Chattanooga, Tenn., *86*
Cheese, from Wisconsin, 100, *121*
Chena River, *5*
Chesapeake Bay, *42*, 43, 95
Cheyenne, Wyo., 102, *102*, 103
Chicago, Ill., 28, *29, 120*
Chisholm Trail, 35
Cincinnati, Ohio, 72, *73*
Clark, George Rogers, 30
Cleveland, Ohio, 72, *73*
Clothing manufacture, in New York, *119*
Coal production
  in Alabama, 3
  in Kentucky, 36
  in West Virginia, 98
  in Wyoming, 103

Coast Guard Academy, 15
Cody, William Frederick, 34, *34*
Colorado, 12, *13*
Colorado River, *6*, *7*, *58*, *89*, *90*
Colorado Springs, Colo., *13*
Columbia, S.C., *83*
Columbia River, 76, 77, 96, 97
Columbus, Ga., *22*
Columbus, Ohio, 72, *73*
Comstock Lode, 59
Concord, Mass., 45, *45*
Concord, N.H., *61*
Congress, U.S., 19
Connecticut, *14*, 15
Connecticut River, *14*, 15, 44, *45*, *61*
Continental Congress, 80, 128
Continental Divide, 12
Copper ore, mined in Utah, 91
Corn crop, Iowa, 33
Cotton crop
    Alabama, 3
    South Carolina, 83
Cotton gin, invention of, 23
Cotton picker, mechanical, *122*
Covington, Ky., *37*
Cranberry crop, Massachusetts, 44
Crater Lake, 76
Craters of the Moon, National Park, 27
Crockett, Davy, 86, 88
Cumberland Gap, 36, *37*
Custer, General, 55

Dallas, Tex., 88
Damien, Father, 111
Danbury, Conn., *14*, 15
Dare, Virginia, 68
Dayton, Ohio, 72, *73*
Deadwood, S.Dak., 85, *85*
Dearborn, Mich., *46*, 47
Death Valley, *10*, 11, 59, *126*, 137
Decatur, Ill., *29*
Declaration of Independence, 19, 78, 79, 80
Delaware, 16, *17*
Delaware Bay, 16, *17*
Delaware River, 16, *17*, *62*, 63, 78
Denver, Colo., 12, *13*
Des Moines, Iowa, *33*
De Soto, Hernando, 8, 9
Du Sable, John Baptiste, 28
Detroit, Mich., 46, *46*, 47
Dew Line, 109
Dinosaur bones, found at Ekalaka, 55
District of Columbia, *18*, 19
Dodge City, Kans., *34*, 35

Dover, Del., *17*
Duluth, Minn., 48, *49*

Earp, Wyatt, 35
Eastport, Me., 40, *41*
Edison, Thomas, 47, 62
Edisto River, *82*
Ekalaka, Mont., 54, 55
Empire State Building, 67
Enterprise, Ala., 3
Erie, Lake, *46*, *66*, 72, *73*, 78
Erie, Pa., *78*
Erie Canal, 67
Eskimo
    kayak of, 4, *126*
    walrus important to, 106
Everglades, Florida, 20, *21*

Fairbanks, Alaska, 4, 5
Fargo, N.Dak., *70*
Fink, Mike, 79
Florida, 20, *21*
Florida Purchase, *129*
Ford, Henry, 46, 47
Forest Rangers, U.S., 54
Fort Knox, Ky., 36, *37*
Fort McHenry, 128
Fort Smith, Ark., *9*
Fort Sumter, 82, *82*
Fort Ticonderoga, *66*, 93
Fort Wayne, Ind., *30*
Fossil remains, 11, 55, 56, 76, 84
Frankfort, Ky., *37*

Gallup, N.Mex., *65*
Galveston, Tex., 88
Gary, Ind., 28, *30*, 31
"General Sherman" (tree), 11, 136
George, Lake (Florida), 20, *21*
Georgia, *22*, 23
Gettysburg, Pa., battleground of, 79
Glacier National Park, 55
Gold Rush
    Alaska, 4, 96
    California, 11
    Colorado, 12, 13
Golden Gate Bridge, 10
Grand Canyon, *6*, 7
Grand Coulee Dam, 96
Grand Forks, N.Dak., *70*
Grand Rapids, Mich., *46*
Great Dismal Swamp, 95
Great Falls, Mont., 54

Great Salt Lake, 90, *90*, 91
Great Smoky Mountains, 68, 87
Green Bay, Wis., 101, *101*
Green Mountain Boys, 93
Greenfield Village, Mich., 47
Groton Naval Base, 15
Gulf of Mexico, *2, 21, 38, 51, 89*

Haidas, 105
Hale, Nathan, 15
Hampton Roads, Va., 95
Hannibal, Mo., 51, *51*
Harrisburg, Pa., *78*
Harrison, Benjamin, 71, 72
Hartford, Conn., *14*
Hawaii, 24, *25*, 110–15, *131*
Hawthorne, Nathaniel, 61
Helena, Mont., *54*, 55
Henry, John, 99
Hialeah Park, 20
Hibbing, Minn., *49*
Hickok, Wild Bill, 85
Homestake Mine, 84
Honolulu, Hawaii, 24, *25*
Hoover, Herbert, 128
Hoover Dam, *125*
Horse farm, Kentucky, 36, *122*
Hot Springs, Ark., *9*
Housatonic River, *14, 45*
Houston, Sam, 88, 89, *89*
Houston, Tex., *89*
Howe, John, 15
Hudson, Henry, 16
Hudson River, *62, 66*
Hula dance, 114
Humboldt River, *58*
Huntington, W.Va., *98*
Huron, Lake, *46*

Idaho, *26*, 27
Illinois, 28, *29*
Illinois River, 28, *29*
Independence Hall, 78, 79
Indiana, *30*, 31
Indianapolis, Ind., *30*, 31
International Falls, *49*
Iowa, 32, *33*
Iron ore production
  in Minnesota, 48
  in Wyoming, 103
Isle Royale, *46*

Jackson, Miss., *50*

Jacksonville, Fla., *21*
Jamestown settlement, 68, 95
Jayne, William, 84
Jefferson City, Mo., *53*
Jefferson Memorial, 19
Jersey City, N.J., *62*, 63
Joliet, Ill., *29*
Jones, John Paul, 43, 128
Juneau, Alaska, *5*, 104

Kahoolawe Island, *25*
Kansas, *34*, 35
Kansas City, Kans., *34*, 35
Kansas City, Mo., 52, *53*
Kauai Island, 24, *25*
Kayak, Eskimo, 4, *126*
Kennebec River, 40, *41*
Kentucky, 36, 37
Kentucky River, 37
Key, Francis Scott, 42, 128
Key West, Fla., 20, *21*
Kipling, Rudyard, 92
Knoxville, Tenn., *86*

La Crosse, Wis., *101*
Lafitte, Jean, 88
Lake Charles, La., *38*, 39
Lanai Island, 24, *25*
Lansing, Mich., *46*
Last Chance Gulch, 55
Las Vegas, Nev., *58*, 59
Lead, S.Dak., 84, *85*
Lead mine, largest, 27, 137
Lewis and Clark Expedition, 8, 56, 70
Lewiston, Me., *41*
Lexington, Mass., 45, *45*
Library of Congress, 19
Liliuokalani, Queen, 112
Lincoln, Abraham, 29, 79, 82, 84
Lincoln, Nebr., 56, *57*
Lincoln Memorial, 19, 23
Little Big Horn River, *54*
Little Blue River, *57*
Little Rock, Ark., *9*
Long, Stephen, 12
Long Island, *66*
Long Island Sound, *14*, 15
Lorain, Ohio, 72, *73*
Los Angeles, Calif., *10*, 11
Louisiana, *38*, 39
Louisiana Purchase, 39, *129*
Louisville, Ky., *37*
Lumber industry
  Maine, 40

Mississippi, 51

Mackinac Straits, *46*, 47
Madison, Wis., *101*
Maine, 40, *41*
Malaspina Glacier, 4, 136–37
Mammoth, fossil remains of, 56
Mammoth Cave, 36, *37*
Mammoth Spring, 8, *9*
Manchester, N.H., *61*
Manhattan Island, sold by Indians, 67
Mardi Gras, New Orleans, 38, *38*, 39
Martha's Vineyard, Mass., *45*
Maryland, *42*, 43
Massachusetts, 44, *45*
Masterson, Bat, 35
Maui Island, 24, *25*, 114
Mauna Kea, 24
Mauna Loa, 24, 115, 136
Memphis, Tenn., *86*
Meriden, Conn., *14*, 15
Meridian, Miss., *50*
Mesabi mine, 136
Meteor Crater, 7
Mexican Cession, *131*
Miami, Fla., 20, *21*
Miami Indians, 31
Michigan, *46*, 47
Michigan, Lake, *29*, *30*, *46*, 101, *101*
Middle Atlantic states, *118–19*
Middle West, *120–21*
Milwaukee, Wis., 100, *101*
Minneapolis, Minn., 48, *49*
Minnesota, 47, 48, *49*
Minuteman, statue of, 45, *45*
Missile Test Center, Air Force, 21
Mississippi, 50, *51*
Mississippi River, 9, 28, *29*, *33*, *34*, *37*, *38*, *49*, *50*, 51, 52, *53*, *86*, 136
Missouri, 52, *53*
Missouri River, *33*, 52, *53*, *54*, *57*, *70*, 84, *85*
Mobile, Ala., *2*, 3
Mojave Desert, *10*, 137
Molokai Island, 24, *25*, 111
Monroe, Wis., 100
Montana, *54*, 55
Montgomery, Ala., *2*
Montpelier, Vt., *93*
Mormons, 59, 91
Morse, Samuel F. B., 43
Morton, J. S., 57
Mount Hood, 76
Mount Katahdin, 40
Mount McKinley, 4, *5*, *108*, 137

Mount Rushmore stone faces, 84
Mount Vernon, 94
Mount Waileale, 136
Mountain states, *124–25*
Movie-making, in Hollywood, 11, *127*
Murfreesboro, Ark., *9*
Muscatine, Iowa, 32, *33*
Muscle Shoals, *2*, 3

Nantucket, Mass., *43*
Nashua, N.H., *61*
Nashville, Tenn., *86*
National Archives building, 19
Nautilus, submarine, 15, *117*
Naval Academy, U.S., 43
Nebraska, 56, *57*
Nevada, *58*, 59
Newark, Del., *17*
Newark, N.J., *62*
New Bedford, Mass., *45*
New England, *116–17*
New Hampshire, 60, *61*
New Haven, Conn., *14*, 15
New Jersey, *62*, 63
New London, Conn., *14*, 15
New Mexico, 12, *64*, *65*
New Orleans, La., 38, 39
New York, *66*, 67
New York City, 66, 67, *118*, 136
Nicolet, Jean, 101
Niihau Island, 25
Norfolk, Va., 94
North Carolina, 68, *69*
North Dakota, *70*, 71
North Platte River, *102*

Oahu Island, 24, *25*
Oakland, Cal., *10*
Oak Ridge, Tenn., 87
Ogden, Utah, *90*
Ohio, 72, *73*
Ohio River, 28, *29*, *30*, *37*, *72*, *73*, 78, *79*, 98
Oil production
    in Oklahoma, 74, 75
    in Wyoming, 103
Okeechobee, Lake, *21*
Okefenokee Swamp, 22, *23*
Oklahoma, *74*, 75
Oklahoma City, Okla., 74, *74*, 75
Old North Church, in Boston, 44, *116*
Olympia, Wash., 97
Omaha, Nebr., 56, *57*
Ontario, Lake, 66

Oregon, 76, 77
Oregon Country Annexation, *130*
Oregon Trail, 77
Ozark Mountains, 9, 52, *53*

Pacific Coast states, *126–27*
Painted Desert, *6, 7*
Pascagoula River, *50,* 51
Pawtucket, R.I., *81*
Peanut crop
   atomic, in North Carolina, 68
  in Georgia, 23, 137
Pearl Harbor, 24
Pearl River, *50,* 51
Pella, Iowa, 32, 33
Penn, William, 79
Pennsylvania, *78,* 79
Penobscot River, *41*
Pensacola, Fla., *21*
Peoria, Ill., *29*
Petrified Forest, 7
Philadelphia, Pa., 78, *78,* 79
Phoenix, Ariz., *6, 7*
Pierre, S.Dak., 84, *85*
Pike, Zebulon, 12, *13*
Pikes Peak, 13
Pilgrims, 44, 68
Pineapple crop, Hawaiian, 24, 113, *126*
Pittsburgh, Pa., *78,* 79
Platte River, 12, 56, *57*
Plymouth Rock, 68
Pocahontas, 95
Pocatello, Idaho, *26*
Polynesians, natives of Hawaii, 110–11
Pony Express, 52
Porcupine Mountains, *46*
Portland, Me., *14*
Portland, Oreg., 77
Potomac River, *18,* 19, *42,* 94, *98*
Pribilof Islands, 106
Providence, R.I., 80
Pueblo, Colo., *13*
Pueblo Indians, 64, 65
Puget Sound, 96

Rainbow Bridge, 91, 136
Raleigh, N.C., *69*
Rapid City, S.Dak., *85*
Red River, *74*
Red River Valley, 71
Reno, Nev., *58*
Revere, Paul, 44
Rhode Island, 80, *81*
Richmond, Va., *94*

Rio Grande, *13,* 64, *65,* 88
Roanoke Island, 68
Roanoke River, *69*
Rochester, Minn., *49*
Rockford, Ill., 27, 28
Rocky Mountains, 12, *13, 26, 54,* 55, *65, 90, 102*
Rodeo, 102, *124*
Roosevelt, Franklin D., 22
Roosevelt, Theodore, 71
Roswell, N.Mex., *65*
Rutland, Vt., *93*

Sacagawea, 70, *70*
Sacramento, Calif., *10*
Sacramento River, *10*
St. Augustine, Fla., 20, *21,* 137
St. Joseph, Mo., 52, *53*
St. Lawrence Seaway, 47, 100, *118*
St. Louis, Mo., 39, 50, 52, *53*
St. Paul, Minn., 48, *49*
Salem, Mass., *45*
Salem, Oreg., 77
Salley, John P., 98
Salmon fishing
  in Alaska, 4
  in Oregon, 76
  in Washington, 96, 97, *97, 127*
Salmon River, *26*
Salt Lake City, Utah, 91
Saluda River, *82*
San Antonio, Tex., 88
San Francisco, Calif., 10, *10,* 11, 52
San Joaquin River, *10*
Sandalwood, 111
Santa Claus, Ind., 31
Santa Fe, N.Mex., 64, *65*
Santee River, *82*
Sarasota, Fla., 20, 21
Sault Sainte Marie, *46*
Saulte Sainte Marie Canal, 47
Savannah, Ga., *22,* 23
Savannah River, *22, 82*
Sea Islands, *22,* 23
Seal, Alaska, 106
Seattle, Wash., 96, 97
Sequoia National Park, 11
Seward, William H., 104
Shawnee Indians, 31
Shenandoah Valley, 99
Shreveport, La., *38*
Sierra Nevada Mountains, 58, *58,* 59
Silver mine, largest, 27, 137
Sioux City, Iowa, *33*
Sioux Falls, S. Dak., *85*

Smith, John, 95
Snake River, *26, 27, 76, 77*
South Bend, Ind., *30*
South Carolina, *82*, 83
South Dakota, 84, *85*
South Platte River, *13*
Southern states, *122–23*
Spokane, Wash., 97
Springfield, Ill., *29*
Springfield, Mass., *45*
"Star-Spangled Banner, The," 42, 128
Statue of Liberty, 67
Steamboats, on Mississippi, 50, *122*
Steel industry
  in Ohio, 72
  in Pennsylvania, 79, *119*
Steubenville, Ohio, 72, *73*
Stevenson, Robert Louis, 111
Sugaring, in Vermont, 92, *117*
Sun Valley, Idaho, 26, *26*
Superior, Lake, 28, *46*, 48, *49, 101*, 136
Supreme Court, 19
Suwannee River, *21*

Tacoma, Wash., 97
Tahoe, Lake, 58, 59
Tallahassee, Fla., *21*
Tampa, Fla., 20, *21*
Tanana, Alaska, 136
Tarpon Springs, Fla., 20, *21*
Tennessee, *86*, 87
Tennessee River, *2, 3, 37, 86*
Tennessee Valley Authority, 87
Texas, 88, *89*
Texas Annexation, *130*
Tidal Basin, *18*
Tlingits, 105
Tobacco crop
  Kentucky, 36
  Virginia, 95
Toledo, Ohio, 72, *73*
Topeka, Kan., *34*
Trenton, N.J., *62*, 63
Tucson, Ariz., *6*
Twain, Mark, 53
Tyler, Tex., 88

Unalaska, 106
United Nations Building, 66, *66*, 92
Uranium production
  in Arizona, 7
  in Colorado, 12
  in New Mexico, 12, 64
  in Wyoming, 103
Uranium prospecting, *125*

Utah, *90*, 91

Valley Forge, 79
Valley of Ten Thousand Smokes, *4, 5*
Vancouver, George, 114
Vandenburg Air Base, 11
Vermont, 92, *93*
Verrazano-Narrows Bridge, 10
Vincennes, Ind., 30
Virginia, *94*, 95
Virginia City, Mont., *54*, 55
Virginia City, Nev., 59
Volcano Observatory, Hawaiian, 115

Wabash River, 28, *29, 30*
Wadsworth, Joseph, 14
War of 1812, 128
Warm Springs Foundation, 22
Washington, 96, 97
Washington, D.C., 18, 19, 23, 43
Washington, George, 19, 63, 79, 94
Waterbury, Conn., 14, 15
West Virginia, *98*, 99
Wheat crop
  Kansas, 35, *120*
  North Dakota, 71
Wheeling, W.Va., 98
White House, *18*
White Mountains, 60, 61, *61*
White River, *13*, 85
White River Badlands, 84
White Sands, N.Mex., 64
Whitney, Eli, 23
Wichita, Kans., *34*, 35
Wilderness Road, 37
Williams, Roger, 80, 81, *81*
Willimantic, Conn., 14, 15
Wilmington, Del., 16, *17*
Winnipesaukee, Lake, *61*
Wisconsin, 100, *101*
Worcester, Mass., 45
Wright, Wilbur and Orville, 69
Wyandotte Cave, 30, 31
Wyoming, *102*, 103

Yampa River, *13*
Yazoo River, *50*
Yellowstone National Park, 103, 137
Yosemite Falls, 137
Young, Brigham, 91
Youngstown, Ohio, 72, *73*
Yukon River, 5

Zion National Park, Utah, 90, 91

Margaret Ronan, who was born in Colorado, has also lived in Wyoming, Montana, New Mexico and Arizona. She is a writer and motion-picture editor for Scholastic Magazines.

Frank Ronan, her husband, has lived in New York State since his arrival from his native Scotland. He is graphics artist for Harper & Row. The Ronans live in Floral Park, on New York's Long Island.

William Meyerriecks, while training as a World War II bomber pilot, was stationed in Massachusetts, Georgia, Florida, Tennessee, Texas, Indiana and Illinois. He is now a free-lance artist living in Huntington, New York.